PAINTING
PORTRAITS

PAINTING
PORTRAITS

25 portrait painting projects illustrated step-by-step
with advice on materials and techniques

Jenny Rodwell

Cincinnati, Ohio

A Quarto Book

Copyright © 1986 Quarto Publishing Ltd
First published in North America by
North Light, an imprint of Writer's Digest Books
9933 Alliance Road
Cincinnati, Ohio 45242

ISBN 0-89134-149-8

This book was designed and produced by
Quarto Publishing Ltd
The Old Brewery, 6 Blundell Street, London N7
9BH

Senior Editor Sandy Shepherd
Art Editor Marnie Searchwell

Editors Jane Rollason, Eleanor Van Zandt

Designer James Culver
Design Assistant Gill Elsbury

Photographer Ian Howes
Photography coordinated by Rob Norridge

Paste-up Graphikos

Art Director Alastair Campbell
Editorial Director Jim Miles

Typeset by Lynne Shippam, QV Typesetting Ltd
Manufactured in Hong Kong by Regent Publishing
Services Ltd
Printed by Leefung-Asco Printers Ltd, Hong Kong

CONTENTS

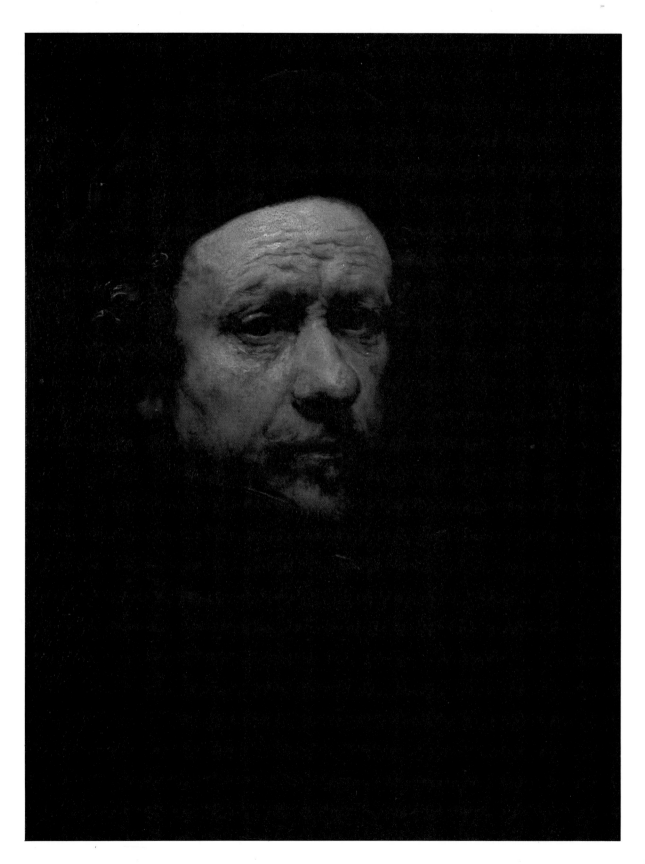

CHAPTER ONE

THE PREPARATION

Portraits involve more preparation and planning than almost any other form of art. When all the sittings have been planned, the pose decided to artist's and sitter's mutual satisfaction, the background chosen and the lighting arranged, then — and only then — can you get on with the real job of drawing or painting the portrait.

Professional portrait painters often spend as much time planning the picture as they do making it. Many artists spend weeks researching and talking to a prospective client. This time is ostensibly spent discussing and planning, but for the artist it is also an opportunity to get to know and observe the subject. The time is rarely wasted. By the time the first sitting takes place, the painter often has firm ideas about how the finished portrait will look.

For most of us such extensive groundwork is unnecessary and impractical, but there is a lot of sense in thinking about the basics before your subject arrives. Whether it is a friend, client or model, it is a waste of their time and yours if you have to spend ages looking for chairs, backgrounds and painting materials during the sitting. So be prepared. This will enable you to devote all your energy and attention to the work in hand as well as making it more enjoyable.

Self-Portrait by Rembrandt (1606-1669). The subject is in a darkened room apparently lit from one direction. Closer scrutiny reveals that the light, however realistic, is not "logical," and the artist has invented highlights to lend emphasis to certain parts of the face.

WHY A PORTRAIT?

If you are asked to do a portrait, either by a friend or as a commission, try to find out what the picture is for. This can often be helpful in deciding what kind of portrait to paint, and can also affect your approach to the work. For instance, if the picture is to be a present, it is useful to know the recipient's taste. If it is a gift for a new home, then it will help to know whether it is to hang alongside antiques or in high-tech surroundings. A family group would probably be done on a large scale, whereas a souvenir portrait or memento for a friend might be better small, even a miniature. Should the pose be formal or informal?

It is always useful to know where the finished portrait will eventually be hung. If you know that, then you know exactly what size to make it.

Don't be afraid of settling these seemingly mundane matters before starting work. It will prevent disappointment, and in the long run will enable you to be more creative rather than less, since you will be free of worry about whether or not your work is suitable.

YOUR SUBJECT

From the outset, it is important to have a good working relationship with your sitter. If you are working on a com-

FORMAL PORTRAIT
Portrait of the Artist's Wife by Thomas Gainsborough (1726-1788), *left*, shows how a formal portrait need be neither stiff or unnatural. The painting of the artist's wife has great warmth and vitality, despite its elegance.

INFORMAL PORTRAIT
The Guitar Player by Jan Vermeer (1632-1675), *above right,* is one of the artist's late works and shows a relaxed, everyday scene in a domestic setting. The subject is not looking at the artist; instead her attention is held by something outside the picture area.

GROUP PORTRAIT
In the *Banquet of the Officers of the Saint George Civic Guard Company* by Frans Hals (1581/5-1666), *right,* the artist solves the problem of composing a portrait of a number of people by not giving prominence to any one of them.

missioned portrait or have been lucky enough to get a friend to sit for you, try not to encroach on their time any more than is absolutely necessary. You can often save time by making sketches or taking photographs. In this way it is possible to keep the sittings to a minimum, filling in background, clothing and so on from these references.

Often a sitter will feel self-conscious, especially if he or she is not used to being painted. It may take a while for your subject to relax, and your own attitude can go a long way in helping to achieve this. If you are nervous and apprehensive, your feelings will almost certainly be passed on; if you are calm and confident, your subject will be reassured and an easy working atmosphere can be established. The first few minutes of each sitting are always slightly tense, and the pose and expression will inevitably change a little. It is not unusual for a pose to start off rigidly upright, only to collapse as the sitter relaxes. Experienced artists always allow for this settling down period.

Many painters talk as they work, encouraging their sitters to do the same. This is usually a deliberate tactic, designed to bring a natural or animated expression to the subject's face. If you find that constant chat affects your concentration, yet you feel uncomfortable with absolute silence, try playing music on a tape or listening to the radio as you work.

Keep the sittings as short as possible and allow plenty of rests during a session. If the pose is particularly tiring, a break every 15 or 20 minutes is a good idea; more comfortable positions can often be held for 45 minutes or an hour. Make sure you mark the subject's position carefully before allowing him or her to move. Use tape or chalk to mark the precise position of the body, hands and even feet, so that the exact pose can be resumed easily after a break. If the chair or couch your sitter is on has to be moved between sessions, mark this also.

FOR PROFIT AND PLEASURE
A professional attitude is essential if you intend to take portrait painting seriously. Even though at the moment you might feel that clients and commissions are problems for the future, it is never too soon to think about the possibilities of extending your interest to reach a wider audience. Most portrait painters begin by painting friends and relatives, building up a reputation slowly as their work becomes known to a wider circle of people. It is important to be reliable and to keep promises, even to members of your own family, completing the work within a given time. Learning your limitations in this way will help you to cope with the more difficult task of working for people that you don't know very well.

If you are working for a fee, settle the details before you start work — however difficult or awkward you find this. It will be far less embarrassing than negotiating a price with the finished portrait in front of you, by which time it can be painfully apparent that you and your subject have widely differing ideas about your artistic worth!

Most successful portrait artists are happier when working to a specific brief, regarding the subject's wishes as a challenge rather than a restriction. Such artists are usually good at their job because they can be creative within certain pre-set limitations. Other painters find working to another person's taste totally intolerable, and would not accept a commission at any price. This attitude is perfectly understandable, and many eminent artists enjoy portraiture for its own sake, doing it to satisfy themselves.

Whether your approach is commercial or otherwise, portrait painting is unlike other painting in that it almost always involves a third party — the subject. Sometimes it is possible to become so immersed in what you are doing that you escape the personality of the sitter, regarding your subject merely as an absorbing arrangement of light, shade, colour and tone. But if you do this, sooner or later your human "still life" will be standing beside you, perhaps saying, "It just isn't me!" As the artist, you have to decide whether this matters to you or not.

THE SETTING
Attitudes to backgrounds vary enormously. Some artists prefer to keep the area behind the sitter as simple as possible, an expanse of neutral tone which does not detract from the sitter in any way. Others choose an appropriate scene or a sketchily painted backcloth which provides a suitable setting but does not dominate the main picture. Some portrait painters consider the background almost as important as the subject itself, revelling in a busy composition filled with minutiae and detail.

The most important thing is to plan the setting carefully as an integral part of the painting, and not to put it in as an afterthought when the rest of the painting is almost finished. Your background should be something you choose, and even if you intend to paint the sitter against a plain wall, the color and tone of the wall should be used to complement the subject. Dark skin, hair and clothing are generally more effective against a light tone, while fair subjects are more suited to a darker background — but you might well decide to reverse this convention. The choice is yours, but it should really be made in the very early stages of planning the portrait.

A collection of drapes and backcloths is invaluable. If you have these on hand, you can quickly try out the various colors, patterns and textures, seeing instantly what the possibilities are. A somber dark background might be best for a formal arrangement, a series of colorful patterns for an informal one. The more alternatives you provide yourself with, the more creative your composition can be.

Space is essential in most portraits. If your subject is painted in three-dimensional terms, with light and shade to suggest the form, then an illusion of space is already created on the canvas. This is why the background is hardly ever painted as a flat color in realistically painted portraits.

A plain wall will usually be graded from light to dark — an indication that normal light never falls evenly — or the subject's shadow will be put in to suggest the space between the figure and the background.

If you plan a complicated background, perhaps an interior or a landscape, the problem of creating space becomes less difficult. Familiar objects, such as trees, buildings and furniture, naturally create spatial relationships, and a three-dimensional environment.

Many people like their portraits to reflect something of themselves in the background. Traditional double portraits, set in appropriate surroundings — usually the sitters' house or garden — are known as conversation pieces. Such paintings hold a special fascination, recording not only the people but also their lifestyle and home environment. Here the background should be chosen carefully, so as to give clues about the subjects' personalities. A favorite armchair or shelf of books, or even a kitchen, can provide an interesting and unusual backdrop for a portrait.

THE RIGHT POSE

The word "pose" is perhaps slightly misleading in this context. It suggests a forced, rather artificial position, whereas the aim of the portrait artist is usually to get a sitter to look as natural as possible. However, it is the word generally used in all portrait and figure work to describe the way in which a subject is presented to the artist.

If your subject is sitting — or perhaps standing — in a position which does not come naturally, you start at a disadvantage, as his, or her, awkwardness will be reflected in your picture. It is worthwhile trying several alternative positions, asking your subject which positions feel right and which don't. A natural position will be more comfortable and will be easier to keep for longer periods of time. In the majority of portraits, the subject is looking directly at the artist. Sometimes the figure is slightly turned to offset the symmetry, but quite often a composition will consist simply of the full-frontal view of a head and shoulders. This kind of approach works well for some artists — usually those whose chief concern is with the character of the subject, and who prefer to focus their attention on the subtle color and texture of the skin, hair and features.

Alternatively, a portrait can be painted in profile, presenting a perfect side view of the subject. This can be parti-

Backgrounds are important in determining the mood of a portrait. In the six pictures, *above*, we see how the color and pattern behind the subject dictate not only the overall effect but also how we perceive the subject; for example, the brown background emphasizes the warm brown tones of the hair and beard.

CHOOSING A POSE
The angle of the head can be crucial to the success of a painting. Traditionally, the portrait poses are, *left to right*, full-face, three-quarters, and profile.

cularly effective if the face possesses prominent, well defined or otherwise distinctive features. A more natural aspect of the face is that which is usually referred to as a three-quarter view. This is halfway between a profile and a full-frontal portrait, and often creates a softer impression of the subject than either of these extremes.

Another important consideration is how much of the subject to include and whether or not you want the hands in the picture. Hands play an important part in the composition of portraits. They echo the tones of the face, often preventing this from standing out as a stark oval, unrelated to the color and tone of the rest of the painting. And they can also be an important part of the composition, guiding the viewer's eyes according to how and where they are placed. Don't shy away from hands just because they might prove difficult. It is surprising how many artists paint hands effectively by dealing with them in the most sketchy and general terms.

Many portraits include a large part of the figure, sometimes the whole top half of the body, and sometimes — usually when the subject is sitting — the legs as well. The main difficulty here is that because the face takes up such a relatively small space compared with everything else, it becomes lost, and you end up with a figure painting instead of a portrait.

WARTS AND ALL!
Society portrait painters often flatter their subjects to a scandalous degree, turning out paintings in which every sitter fits into the fashion type of the moment — whatever his or her actual size, shape or coloring might be. Such flagrant disregard for the evidence of the eyes is doubtless a lucrative pursuit, but the result is usually sterile, painted

to a formula, and deserving of the label it is often given — chocolate-box art.

It is not difficult to paint away unwanted flesh, put a youthful twinkle in the eye, or soften the contours of the face, but it is difficult to produce a worthwhile portrait in this way. A good likeness is the indirect result of honest observation and can best be achieved by concentrating on the basic structure and main forms within the subject rather than attending to superficial detail.

LIGHTING
Most artists prefer working by natural light if this is at all possible. A northern light is the best, providing a clear, constant light source which does not cast heavy, changing shadows across the sitter's face. Light from other directions is subject to shadows and reflections, a southerly light being the most difficult of all to work by. All natural light is short-lived and inconsistent, increasing and diminishing throughout the day. For this reason many artists prefer to paint entirely by artificial lighting, secure in the knowledge that they can work when and where they please.

Modern fluorescent "daylight" bulbs are an excellent substitute for the real thing. They can be used in place of natural lighting, or can be arranged across a window and used to replace the daylight as it fades and changes. Artists who depend solely on artificial lighting often use a strong main lamp and supplement this with fill-in lights to counteract the strong directional beam from the main source.

An alternative method is to use a main light source and reflector screens, sheets of white which produce a soft, reflected glow on the subject's face. By placing a screen opposite the main light source, you can illuminate one side of the face quite dramatically and use the screen gently to light the other side, thus avoiding harsh contrasting areas of light and shade.

Since the Renaissance, Western art has nearly always used light and shade to describe the contours and form of the subject. The portraits of Leonardo da Vinci (1452-1519) are illuminated by a broad light from above. He realized that the closer the lighting resembled natural sunlight, the more realistic and convincing the painting would be. Light from above is the light by which most of us recognize people we know, and indeed, as Leonardo pointed out to his contemporaries, if you met a close friend "lit from below you would find it difficult to recognize him".

Other artists have deliberately chosen unnatural or dramatic lighting for the special atmosphere it can create. Joseph Wright of Derby (1734-97) specialized in lighting effects. His dramatic scenes, often illuminated by moonlight or candlelight, are reminiscent of many seventeenth-century Dutch painters, who in turn took their lead from the Italian artist, Michelangelo Caravaggio (1573-1610).

Caravaggio used an emphatic balance of light and shade to create movement and volume in his painting. The technique is known as chiaroscuro (in French it is *clair obscur*) and the portraits and figures created in this way often seem to have been literally sculpted out of a dark, shadowy background and to catch the light as they come to the surface.

Different lighting techniques tend to become associated with the portrait painters who employ them. Often the lighting in a painting can look completely natural, but on close observation we realize it can only be either the result of an intricate lighting system or the product of a fertile imagination. Rembrandt (1606-69), who has probably had more influence in the field of portrait painting than any other artist, used light in just such a way. He introduced highlights to emphasize a particular contour or area of the face, regardless of logic or of the probability of such effects occurring in real life.

Bending the rules of nature is fine and there is nothing wrong with taking a little artistic licence in the interests of creating a more interesting painting, but it can be overdone. Too much fragmented light and over-zealous highlighting will soon destroy what it was intended to achieve. Instead of describing the contours and volumes it can eventually flatten them. Always try to see your subject in general terms, using broad planes of light and shade, at least until the basic form is established.

LIGHTING

In everyday life we see the human face in a complexity of simultaneous light sources. For the beginner, it is a good idea to limit the light sources, and later to experiment by changing or strengthening them. The effects here, *above*, were achieved with a combination of direct, artificial lights.

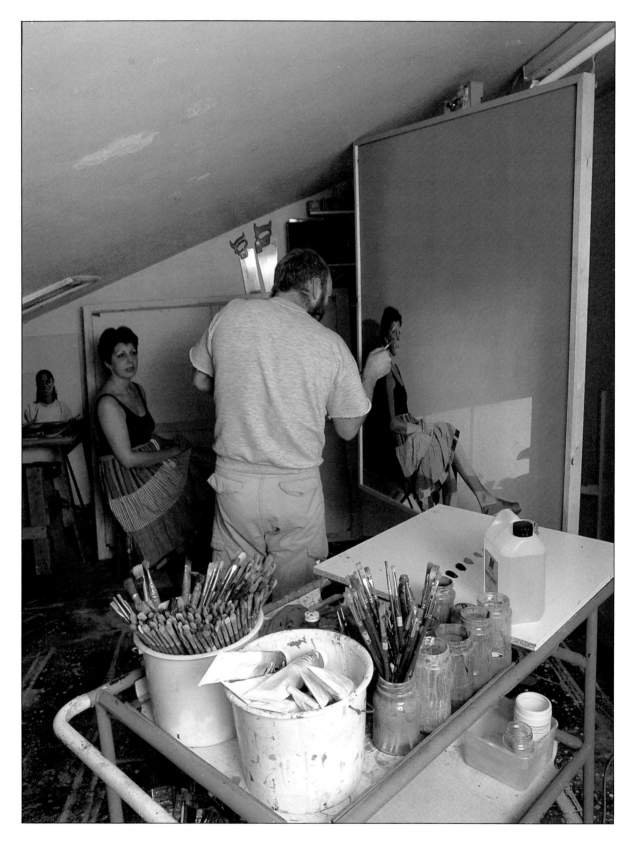

CHAPTER TWO

MATERIALS

Portrait painting can be divided into two distinct categories — those done in the studio and those painted on location. Working in the studio gives you the advantage of familiarity, of knowing where everything is, and of being in control of the environment. Painting away from base is often unavoidable, and although it can also be stimulating and exciting, it usually gives you less control over the situation — the lighting, background and general working atmosphere. In such cases you will need to plan carefully and take some special items of equipment.

This chapter looks at some basic materials and tools, paying particular attention to the special requirements of working away from the studio. Where possible, I suggest inexpensive alternatives to professional equipment.

The professional portrait painter's studio, *left*, is well-ordered and convenient — a workshop where equipment and materials are at hand, and where both artist and sitter can feel at ease. North-facing overhead windows eliminate harsh shadows and keep the problem of changing light to a minimum.

IN THE STUDIO

The professional portrait artist's studio is usually a highly organized workshop, arranged in such a way as to provide a convenient and relaxed environment with as few distractions and irritations as possible. It is a place where a model or sitter can feel at home, and where the artist can work in comfort with all the materials at hand, thus avoiding disruptive and time-consuming rummaging and searching during painting sessions.

Whether you are lucky enough to have a studio or room set aside specially for painting, or whether your working space is a more temporary affair — perhaps a makeshift space in the living area of your home — an orderly approach is essential. Time is precious, and when the subject is there in front of you, the more time spent in direct observation and painting the better. Many artists, once they know the basic skin color of the subject, actually have a range of general flesh tones mixed on the palette before the session starts, adjusting these slightly to fit the specific requirements.

Labeled filing cabinets, chests of drawers and office storage systems can be used to keep paints, brushes and other materials in an orderly way which does not impinge on the working environment. A trolley for holding those materials currently in use can organize your working area and can be pushed aside when not needed.

THE MODEL STAND

Most portraits are painted with the subject seated, for obvious reasons. The majority of portrait painters work standing, to enable them to stand back from their work and make an occasional overall assessment of it. Unless the artist wants to see his or her subject from this high vantage point, with a good view of the top of the head, the subject must be raised approximately to the painter's eye level. The professional way of doing this is to use a model stand, a platform which is large enough and strong enough to take the weight of the model and a chair or sofa.

A suitable stand can be made from wood or by cutting down the legs of an unwanted, sturdy old table. Or you can improvise by using planks of wood across blocks or bricks, providing these are stable enough to carry the weight. For quick sketches and paintings, a high stool will often suffice, although this offers no support for the subject's back and will be too uncomfortable for long sittings.

FRENCH OR BOX EASEL

WATERCOLOR OR SKETCHING EASELS

DRAPES AND SCREENS

A selection of background drapes is invaluable. Keep a collection of old sheets and curtains, solid-color and patterned, so that you have a choice of background for every portrait you paint. There is no need to be restricted by the color of the wall or the accidental surroundings of your studio just because they happen to be there.

The color of the sitter's skin and hair will often suggest the tone and color of background required, and what the subject is wearing will usually dictate whether this should be solid or patterned. You may decide on a totally plain composition, perhaps predominantly white or black, or you might choose a cacophony of color and conflicting patterns. Either way, you will be limited by the materials available, so the more choice you have, the more exciting and interesting your composition will be.

Background drapes can be pinned to the wall, although a more portable device provides greater scope. Folding screens — the type used in hospitals — are ideal because they can be adjusted to the required shape. Metal clothes

LARGE STUDIO EASEL

DONKEY

RADIAL EASEL

racks, used in some boutiques and thrift shops, are a good alternative. Keep a stock of paper clips, bulldog clips and safety pins to secure the drapes in place.

EASELS

A large studio easel provides the best support for large canvases and boards. Its size and bulk, however, limits its use to the permanent studio rather than the "occasional" painting space.

A good alternative to the studio easel is the more manageable radial easel. Again, this offers quite adequate support for most canvases and drawing boards, and has the added advantage of being foldable. This makes it easy to store, although it is still usually considered too heavy and cumbersome for extensive painting trips, painting outdoors and location work.

If you prefer to work sitting down, the artist's "donkey" provides both a seat and a support for your work. This type of easel does not allow free movement for the artist, however, and has the disadvantage of making it difficult to

move back and see the work from a distance. It is also fairly low and — for the portrait painter — generally offers a restricted view of the subject.

The table easel is a useful, compact piece of equipment for smaller paintings and drawings, if you have a suitable desk or table to work on.

For watercolor painters, an adjustable watercolor easel is essential. Various models are available, made in metal or wood. These can be adjusted to a horizontal position to allow areas of wet paint and wash to be applied without the color running down the paper.

AWAY FROM THE STUDIO

Many people prefer their portrait to be painted in their own home. In some cases this is because they want the background in the painting to reflect their personality, and thus wish to be surrounded by their own furniture and familiar objects. Other people find an artist's studio intimidating, while for some — especially elderly people — going out may be difficult or impossible.

17

Working in new places can be challenging, forcing you to take a fresh look at new backgrounds in unfamiliar lighting conditions. It can also counteract complacency, "blowing away the cobwebs" and getting rid of a certain staleness which inevitably occurs if you paint the same situation time and time again. The success of your painting trip will depend largely on how you plan it, and on having the right equipment to cope with it. Make a list of everything you are likely to need from the large items of equipment down to old rags and tissues – and take it all. There is nothing more detrimental to confidence or concentration than the insecurity which comes from the feeling of having forgotten something.

CARRYING PAINTING GEAR

Portable painting sets are excellent. If the bought ones are too small for all your materials, a wooden box with a handle can be adapted to your personal needs. If you are using oils, acrylic or watercolor, plastic jars with screw lids are ideal for carrying water or any other medium.

Paintbrushes travel badly, especially soft watercolor brushes. If possible, keep the plastic protector caps which come with most new brushes and use these to prevent the bristles from getting damaged. Lightweight metal and plastic tubular brush cases are available from artists' suppliers; these should be carried upright to preserve the shape of the bristles.

Wet canvases can present a problem unless you make provision for carrying them. Almost-dry pictures can sometimes be covered in newspaper, but this often flattens the texture and deadens the surface. A better idea is to equip yourself with a special clamp or with a set of four canvas separators, also available from artists' suppliers. Both these carrying devices work by holding two surfaces apart, and require two canvases or boards of the same size.

PORTABLE EASELS

Lightweight, portable sketching easels are adequate for small and medium-sized canvases or boards. These come in metal or wood and are specially designed for the peripatetic painter. If you plan a larger painting, then a folding studio easel – a cross between a sketching easel and the bulky radial easel – could be the answer.

Sketch box easels have a useful compartment for paints, brushes and rags. This type of easel collapses into a handy carrying case and often incorporates its own palette.

Whichever easel you choose, buy the best you can afford. It will last a lifetime and is a good investment. Many artists can boast of easels which belonged to their grandparents and great-grandparents and which will very likely be used by generations to come.

MATERIALS

It is all too easy to be intimidated by the vast choice of materials and equipment now available. Most artists' supply shops, though fascinating and wondrous places to browse in, seem frightening and inhospitable when it comes to selecting and paying for the materials you want – or think you want!

The first rule is to start with the minimum. There may well be an enormous range to choose from, but that doesn't mean you have to buy every single item. This book introduces most of the materials you will need and gives advice on how to control costs, by buying only what is necessary and adding to these basics as your experience and confidence increase.

DRAWING MATERIALS

Most portrait painters make drawings and sketches before committing the image to the canvas. This not only helps with the technical problems of the picture, with the com-

WATERCOLOR

GOUACHE

18

position, tone, structure and so on, but also gives the artist a precious opportunity to become familiar with the character and facial expressions of the subject. Almost any medium can be used, depending on the artist and the method of working.

If a painting is particularly complicated, several preliminary sketches may be necessary. A group portrait can be assembled from a series of individual sketches, by means of changing and experimenting with the order of the components until the right composition emerges. Choose the materials according to your requirement. Pastels and colored pencils are useful for making quick color sketches; chalk and charcoal, for establishing the light and shade; pencil or pen and ink, for form, line and detail.

Drawing is invaluable for preliminary and exploratory work, but it can also be an end in itself. Finished portraits are not necessarily painted ones — some of the finest portraits ever done are drawings. Leonardo da Vinci drew portraits in ink, chalk and silverpoint. Contemporary artists have used colored pencils, felt-tipped pens and children's wax crayons with great success.

There is no restriction on your choice of drawing materials, and it is important for you to feel free to experiment, discovering your own favorites and combining different media to get the effect you want. Portraits can be done in any medium, including pencil, pen, pastel and a wide variety of lesser-known drawing materials. Most drawing equipment is relatively inexpensive and offers ample opportunity to develop your skills without feeling inhibited by cost.

PAINTS

Traditional painting media are oils, watercolor and gouache. Acrylic is a relatively new paint, but is becoming increasingly popular for portrait painting.

Oil, the most common painting medium, is slow-drying and can be moved and manipulated on the support for several hours before it dries. Its potential is enormous, and it can be used in an almost infinite number of ways. Artists whose styles and attitudes are intrinsically different in every other respect often have this medium in common. The paint can be used thickly, either with a knife or brush, or it can be diluted and applied in layers of thin glazes. Portrait painters have exploited both methods, but the technique of glazing, building up layer upon layer of transparent color, is particularly effective when painting skin tones.

Acrylic paints are extremely quick-drying and very durable. The medium has not yet been fully explored, and suffers from unfair comparison with other paints. The color, once laid, cannot easily be moved or changed, and demands a different approach from that needed with either oil or watercolor.

Watercolor can be applied loosely, with free washes and expressive brushstrokes, or it can be used quite tightly for highly finished portraits. Practice and patience are needed to get the best results from this medium, but these are richly rewarded by the characteristic transparency and delicacy of watercolor effects.

Gouache is an opaque form of watercolor. It is a lively, spontaneous medium, equally suited to both quick color sketches and more exacting work. Many portrait painters have taken advantage of the immediacy of the medium to capture the fleeting expressions and short-lived poses of their subjects.

The projects in the later chapters of this book include paintings done in each of these media. Their differences and the many effects possible with each of the paints can be seen in the finished pictures, with demonstrations of the techniques used to achieve them.

ACRYLIC

OIL PASTELS

TECHNICAL PEN

WATERCOLOR PENCILS

TEMPORAL BONE

CHEEK BONE

MASTOID PROCESS

UPPER JAW

LOWER JAW

NECK VERTEBRAE

BREAST BONE
COLLAR BONE

TEMPORAL MUSCLE

ORBICULARIS OCULI (AROUND THE EYE)

CHEEK BONE

MASSETER MUSCLE (FOR CHEWING)

LEVATOR MUSCLES (LIFT CORNERS OF MOUTH)

ORBICULARIS ORIS (CONTROLS THE LIPS)

DEPRESSOR MUSCLE (PULLS DOWN CORNERS OF MOUTH)

MASTOID MUSCLE

TRAPEZIUS MUSCLE

COLLAR BONE

MAJOR PECTORAL MUSCLE

DELTOID MUSCLE

BREAST BONE

BICEPS

CHAPTER THREE

ANATOMY
FOR THE
PORTRAIT ARTIST

Portraiture is infinitely easier if you have some idea of what lies beneath the face of the subject. Obviously it is not necessary to remember the name of every bone and muscle, but a working knowledge of how they function and their effect on the external form and shape of the subject can be a great help.

The sketchbooks of Leonardo da Vinci demonstrate a depth of understanding and knowledge of the human body which was unique in his own lifetime and which few artists possess today, despite the advanced technical and medical material now available. Leonardo's faces reflect a lifelong interest in anatomy, and the deep sympathy and humanity of his portrait drawings and paintings are more a product of an accurate understanding of the underlying structure than of any inspired insight into his subjects.

Facial expressions are not "stuck" onto the surface of the face. A smile or grimace cannot be portrayed by merely making the corners of the mouth turn up or down. These expressions are muscular movements which affect not only the mouth, but the whole of the face, so to paint a convincing smile, you must also paint a smiling jaw, nose, eyes and forehead! And to do this, you must understand the muscles that lie beneath the surface of the skin.

Every portrait painter should have a basic knowledge of anatomy — of the bones and muscles that lie under the skin. The drawings on the opposite page show the bones of the head, neck, and shoulders, *top left*; the muscles and ligaments, *bottom*; and the head complete with skin and hair, *top right*.

THE SKULL

A human skull is made up of two parts — the cranium, which encloses the brain, and the jaws. Surprisingly, there are 22 bones in the skull, eight of which form the cranium. It is not important for the artist to know exactly what, or even where, all these bones are, but it is useful to know something about them.

The shape of the cranium dictates the shape of the head. It varies considerably in different individuals, but is roughly oval whether viewed from the top or from the side. Its shape also varies between individuals.

It is helpful to think of the cranium as having a roof, or vault, which covers the top of the head, and a base, which is completely covered by the face and neck. The roof is thicker than the sides, being made up of two layers of bone with a spongy bone layer sandwiched between them. More vulnerable is the thin, translucent bone which makes up the sides of the cranium. Although this structure is often totally hidden under a thick head of hair, it is important to remember that the shape of the hair is partly dictated by the shape of the cranium underneath.

In young babies the cranium is much larger in relation to the face than in older children or adults. The distance from the top of the eye sockets to the lower edge of the jaw accounts for half of a baby's head length, but in adults it takes up about two-thirds. Within the first year of the child's life the bones of the cranium grow and fuse together and the jaw becomes more prominent as the face and features mature.

THE JAWBONES

The bones of the face and cranium are firmly joined to one another, with the exception of the lower jawbone, or mandible. In newborn babies the mandible consists of two halves. These meet at the chin and join together in early infancy to form one bone. This is hinged to the cranium just in front of the ear. The upper jaw, which is fixed, consists throughout life of two separate bones — the *maxillae*. Each *maxilla* forms half the roof of the mouth, much of the side of the nose, and the hard bony base of the eye socket. Thus, to a large extent the *maxillae* dictate the shape of the upper part of the face.

Newborn babies have small, undeveloped lower jaws in relation to the rest of the face. When the teeth begin to grow, the jaw expands to accommodate these, becoming

FACIAL EXPRESSIONS
Our feelings and reactions are reflected in our faces. Anger, *above*, distorts the facial muscles; the scowling man uses the forehead muscles to furrow his brow, and his nose and cheek muscles to wrinkle his nose.

more prominent and so lengthening the shape of the whole face. Adult bones, once formed, do not change significantly in shape, although their position may change in relation to each other. This is because adjoining cartilage dries in old age, causing a shrunken look. In the skull, the loss of teeth causes the jaw to recede.

THE MUSCLES

Facial expressions are made by the muscles moving under the skin of the face, scalp and neck. It is difficult to move any one of these muscles without affecting its neighbors — as we find if we try to raise an eyebrow or wink at someone without distorting the rest of our face. Although most of us know someone who boasts of being able to wiggle his ears, wobble his scalp or twitch his nose, these feats require much practice and are beyond the capabilities of most people. To the majority of us, the expression "pulling a face" means exactly what it says, pulling and stretching the muscles to make a particular facial expression.

We use muscles to close and open our eyes and mouth, to speak and eat, even to sniff. The muscles, therefore, are directly related to the orifices — the mouth, eyes and nose.

The muscles around the mouth are particularly important to the portrait painter. They are responsible for the movement of the lips and are the reason why the mouth stands considerably proud of the lower half of the face — a fact often overlooked by inexperienced artists, many of whom paint the lips directly on to a mistakenly flattened face. This "mound" beneath the mouth, the *orbicularis oris,* is made up of several muscles which enter the lips from below and above. Another muscle called the buccinator passes horizontally from the corner of the mouth and into the cheek.

Surrounding the cavity of each eye, and allowing the eye to close tightly or gently, is the *orbicularis oculi* muscle. The eyes can also be moved indirectly by the large, flat muscles which run from the top of the scalp through the forehead. You can demonstrate this by tightly creasing your forehead, noticing how it inevitably widens the eyes, and by moving the nose.

The neck and shoulders are of great importance to the portrait artist. How the head is attached to the neck, and how the neck movement affects the head, are crucial to the pose and how you perceive it. An upward or sideways tilt of the chin must always be accompanied by a corresponding tension in the neck, however slight. The ability to notice and interpret these subtle movements is a quality which you, as a portrait painter, should aim to develop. Such observation can create the difference between a living likeness and a wooden-looking portrait which captures nothing of the vitality, character or pose of the sitter.

The most important muscle in the neck passes from behind the ears to the inside of the clavicle. This muscle,

the sternocleidomastoid muscle, is situated on both sides of the neck and enables the head and neck to bend forward and the head to turn from side to side. The neck should never be overlooked. It is far from being an uninteresting piece of flesh which joins the head to the body. Many people have well-developed neck muscles, which can be elegant, sinewy, solid or scraggy. If you overlook these particular characteristics, you will lose an important key to the final likeness.

Your knowledge of anatomy will be of use only if you can put it into practice. Obviously if you know where the *orbicularis oculi* is, but not what it looks like, then merely knowing the name isn't going to help you draw or paint it. One excellent way of learning practical anatomy is to observe yourself in a mirror. Make faces, move your head from side to side, and try out various poses and expressions. Notice which muscles you use and how they look, making sketches if necessary to help you to remember. You will be surprised how quickly you become familiar with the structure underneath the skin.

CHAPTER FOUR

MIXING COLOR

Whether you are using oil, acrylic, watercolor, pastel or colored pencils for your portraits, it is helpful to have a basic understanding of color theory and to know a little about how to mix the different pigments. In the case of paints, and sometimes pastels, each color has a name, making it easier to learn and remember the various color combinations. Pencils are usually identified by a number only, so it is a question of finding and identifying equivalent colors.

Almost all painting and drawing media come in a wide range of colors, and you will always be able to find the exact one you want. The problem is more likely to be one of deciding which colors to leave out. For the novice who has not yet developed a personal color range, it is an enormous temptation to try to use every possible color simply because they look so beautiful when they are laid out side by side in the shop or as they appear on the color chart. The result is almost always disappointing. It is far better to start with a few colors, increasing these as you become familiar with the media and as your technique improves to accommodate a more complex palette. The fewer colors you use, the more you are forced to mix them, and the greater the chance of pictorial harmony as each color is repeated throughout the whole composition.

There is no "correct" way of painting flesh tones. In the four portraits *opposite* we see some of the ways in which different artists tackle the subject, and the colors they used.

When you choose your materials, remember that no colors can be mixed to make the primaries — red, yellow and blue — and that it is quite possible to work with these three colors alone, with the addition of white. Use the primary colors as your starting point, adding gradually to these as the need arises. Every artist develops a personal preference for certain colors, and you will find it helpful to note which colors the artists used in the step-by-step portraits in the later chapters of this book. Only by mixing and using colors is it really possible to become acquainted with the properties of the different pigments. There are no rules to go by, and only experience will determine which rules are right for you.

PRIMARIES, SECONDARIES AND TERTIARIES

The primary colors are red, blue and yellow. Cadmium red, cadmium yellow and ultramarine blue are the pigments that come closest to the pure primaries, and these are to be found on most artists' palettes. Secondary colors are mixed from two primaries: blue and red make violet, yellow and blue make green, and yellow and red make orange. It should not be essential to have these colors because you can mix them yourself from red, yellow and blue. However, the theory of color is based on the colors of the spectrum, which are pure, but artists' colors behave differently, as you will see if you try to mix violet from cadmium red and ultramarine blue. The result will be a muddy, purplish brown. For this reason, painters often prefer to buy the proprietary equivalent of the secondary colors, choosing bright oranges, violets and greens to suit their purpose.

Tertiary colors are those created from mixing a primary and a secondary color together. For example, blue and green combine to make a bluish green, red and orange to make a reddish orange and so on.

COMPLEMENTARY COLORS

Primary, secondary and tertiary colors are often arranged in a wheel — the so-called color wheel. Those pairs of colors which fall opposite each other in the wheel are known as "complementary." Thus, orange and blue, red and green, and blue and yellow are all complementary to each other. It is useful to remember these because they have a practical application. One of the best ways to subdue or reduce the brightness of a color without causing it to go gray is to mix it with a little of its complementary. Alternatively, any color can be made to look brighter on the canvas by placing it next to its complementary.

TONAL VALUE

Every color has a tonal value. If you can imagine how a color would look in a black and white photograph, you are close to understanding its tonal value. Yellow, for instance, photographs as a light gray and therefore has a high tonal value; dark red or blue reproduces as dark gray, and has a low or dark tonal value. The tonal, or achromatic, scale ranges from black to white, and every color has a gray equivalent somewhere between those two extremes. It is important to understand how tone works because it affects the way you use color, and even the most brightly colored composition can look flat if it lacks tonal contrast.

Many artists make a "tonal" drawing of their subject before starting work, to establish the light and dark areas. This can be done in pencil, charcoal, or white paint used with black or one other color. Good lighting can also dictate the tonal interest in a portrait because it creates contrasting planes of light and shade across the subject's face and elsewhere in the composition. A background that is lighter or darker than the subject's hair or clothing can often help to vary the tonal pattern of a portrait and it is worthwhile experimenting with different combinations.

HUE AND INTENSITY

The actual color of a pigment is known as the "hue." When we talk of yellow, green or red, for example, what we are actually referring to is the hue. When we describe the brightness of a particular color, we refer to the "intensity"

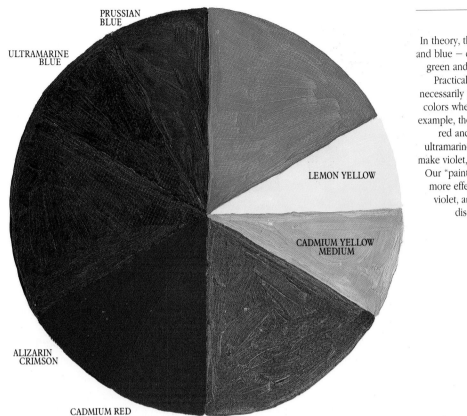

PRUSSIAN BLUE

ULTRAMARINE BLUE

LEMON YELLOW

CADMIUM YELLOW MEDIUM

ALIZARIN CRIMSON

CADMIUM RED

(occasionally called "chroma") of that color. Again, it is the practical application which is important, not the terminology, and you will know whether or not your color is bright enough by how it looks in the painting.

SOME BASIC COLORS

The following list is not comprehensive, but provides a guide to some of the basic colors used by many portrait painters. The colors apply to oils and watercolor. Acrylics sometimes have the same name, but in some cases they are different. The acrylic name, or the equivalent acrylic color is given in parentheses where relevant.

Cadmium red. Cadmium red medium is close to primary red. Cadmium light and dark are versions of the same color. They are opaque and mix well with yellow to make orange, making them almost essential for bright, warm flesh tones. The cadmium reds cannot be mixed with blue to make violet and purple:

Alizarin (phthalocyanine crimson). A cool, bluish red often used with ultramarine blue to mix cool, purplish flesh shadows. Also mixes with white to make basic pink.

Rose (naphthol crimson). A vivid pinkish red is a useful addition to the portrait painter's palette. Different manufacturers produce different versions under different names (Rowney Rose is one example in the oil-paint range). Rose, geranium, madder and magenta are all good

The tonal scale, *left*, runs from black to white, and every color has a tonal equivalent somewhere on that scale.

Some of the most popular colors are shown here *right*. The list is not comprehensive, but offers an extensive range from which you can select your initial palette. Names apply to oil or watercolor. Where the acrylic name differs, the name of the equivalent acrylic color is given in parentheses.

CADMIUM RED   ALIZARIN (PHTHALOCYANINE CRIMSON)   ROSE (NAPHTHOL CRIMSON)   CADMIUM ORANGE   CHROME ORANGE   ULTRAMARINE BLUE

CHROMIUM OXIDE   COBALT VIOLET (DIOXAZINE PURPLE)   TERRE VERTE   VIRIDIAN (PHTHALOCYANINE GREEN)   SAP GREEN   WHITE

strong pink reds, although the precise names vary according to the medium you are working in.

Cadmium orange. A bright orange, premixed from cadmium reds and yellow.

Chrome orange. Vivid orange with strong tinting power. Cheaper than cadmium orange, but should be regarded as an alternative in certain cases only, because it is considered incompatible with the cadmium colors.

Ultramarine blue. Regarded as the "primary" blue, ultramarine is used by nearly all artists. It can be mixed with crimson and pink reds to make purples and violets, and is often used in the cooler skin tones.

Monestial blue (phthalocyanine blue). Cold, bright blue with very strong tinting power. Monestial blue must be used sparingly if it is not to dominate other colors. Makes purple when mixed with crimson and pink reds, and bright greens when mixed with yellow.

Cobalt blue. Particularly popular with portrait painters for the cool shadows it produces, cobalt blue is subtle without being particularly opaque or stongly tinted.

Cerulean blue. A gentle, sky blue used for its opacity and distinctive color.

Cadmium yellow. This standard, primary yellow is used for making strong greens and oranges when mixed with blue and red respectively. It is strong and opaque and comes in three tones — light, medium and dark.

Lemon yellow. A light, cool yellow with slightly weaker tinting power than the cadmiums. Transparent and clear, it can be used to mix vivid oranges and greens.

Yellow ocher (yellow oxide). Used by the majority of portrait painters, this dull, dark yellow is fairly opaque and almost essential for making white flesh tones, when it is often mixed with burnt sienna, white and a little blue.

Hooker's green. A subtle green which mixes well with earth pigments, it is traditionally a landscape color, but is also used by many portrait painters.

Chromium oxide. This dull grey-green is opaque and occasionally used for the underpainting of flesh tones.

Cobalt violet (dioxazine purple). A strong, pre-mixed violet useful in cool white flesh tones.

Terre verte. A dull green traditionally used for underpainting flesh tones.

Viridian (phthalocyanine green). A vivid, darkish green sometimes used in cool skin tones.

Sap green. A rich green usually used by landscape artists but occasionally found on the portrait painter's palette.

Indian red. A deep brick red, sometimes used in flesh tones when a more dominant red is not required.

Raw umber. Often used instead of black to tone down other color, raw umber is found on the majority of artists' palettes. Its yellow-brown pigment has relatively poor tinting power.

Burnt umber. This warm brown is used mainly for mixing with other colors to produce a range of rich tones. It is reasonably opaque.

Raw sienna. A fairly opaque, sandy color, raw sienna is a mixture of ocher, orange and brown. When mixed with greens, blues and purples, it produces a range of rich earth tones suitable for many subjects.

Burnt sienna. A warm, transparent color which is often used for glazing flesh tones. It is rich and coppery, usually used when a bright red is not wanted.

MONESTIAL BLUE (PHTHALOCYANINE BLUE)   COBALT BLUE   CERULEAN BLUE   CADMIUM YELLOW   LEMON YELLOW   YELLOW OCHER (YELLOW OXIDE)   HOOKER'S GREEN

INDIAN RED   RAW UMBER   BURNT UMBER   RAW SIENNA   BURNT SIENNA   PAYNE'S GRAY   IVORY BLACK

Payne's gray. A cold, dark gray, this is often used instead of black. Payne's gray is especially useful for modifying other colors.

Titanium white. An opaque white with good covering power. Only a small amount of titanium white is necessary to lighten a color, thus preserving the transparency of the color.

Ivory black. A popular, dense black which should be used sparingly for mixing. Many artists use no black at all, preferring to darken color with an alternative dark pigment, such as raw umber.

PAINTING FLESH TONES

Sadly, there is no magic formula for painting the color of human flesh. In the above list we have mentioned those pigments popularly used by many artists, but the choice is ultimately a personal one, depending on experience and your approach to the subject. For white-skinned subjects you will obviously need white, a red and a yellow, plus a green or blue to produce the cool shadow areas. But, as you will see from the paintings in this book, the options are extremely wide because skin color varies from person to person, and the possible combinations are endless.

A good basic range of colors for a portrait painter to start with would possibly be white, black, chromium oxide, cerulean blue, ultramarine blue, alizarin crimson, light red, cadmium red, raw umber, burnt sienna, raw sienna, cadmium yellow and yellow ocher. Many painters work with far fewer colors, and you may eventually find that some of these are superfluous. Above all, do not be frightened of experimenting and introducing new variations to your palette.

Professional portrait painters are usually highly organized when mixing flesh tones. The local color of a subject's face usually varies very little, though the tonal differences created by lighting can be enormous, ranging not only from light to dark, but also from warm to cool. Shadows tend to be cool; illuminated areas are generally warmer. Artists often prefer to mix an approximate range of these visible tones at the outset, adding to these where necessary, instead of trying to mix each new tone separately as the need arises. The planes of the face are rounded, subtle and undefined, each area of tone merging into the next in an almost indiscernible way. To mix every tone as you come to it is to make a difficult task into an almost impossible one!

Some modern portrait painters have exaggerated the subtle tones found in the skin without forfeiting either the likeness or the character of the subject. Such interpretation can often enhance the image, underlining and emphasizing those characteristics which the artist wishes to draw attention to. Van Gogh's self-portraits are far from being straightforward color copies of his own face. Henri Matisse (1869-1934), in his *Portrait of André Derain*, chose the Fauvist approach of expressive brushstrokes and intense color, juxtaposing brilliant viridian shadows against cadmium orange and red flesh tones.

As you will see from the way the artists in this book work, there is no single "correct" approach to painting or drawing flesh. Every artist approaches the subject in a different way, and it would be a pity if you restricted yourself without first trying the alternatives.

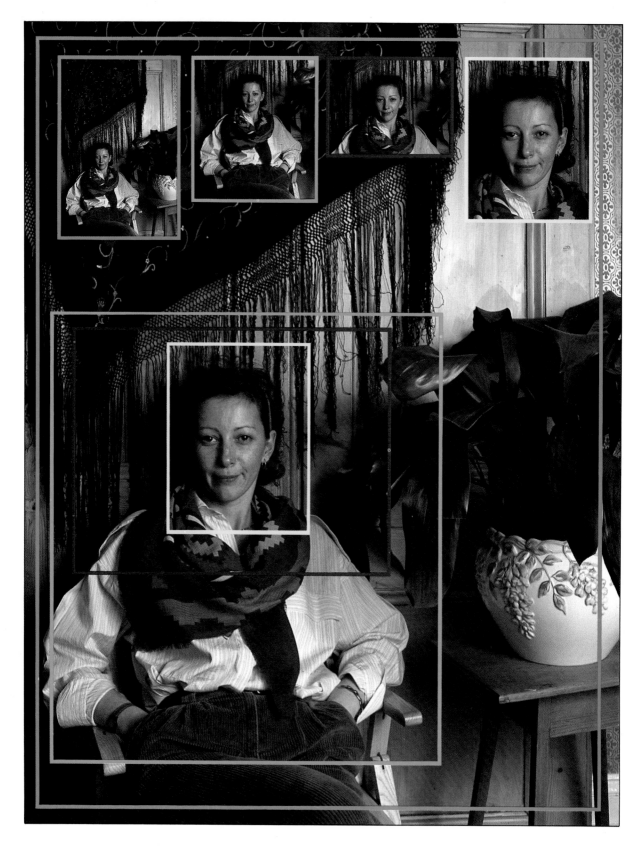

CHAPTER FIVE

THE
PORTRAIT

Composition is an important element in any painting; even a seemingly simple head-and-shoulders portrait needs to be "composed" to some extent if it is to suceed, while the scale of the picture is another vital consideration. Sketches and photographs are both useful in helping to organize the portrait in advance, so that you do not waste valuable painting time by changing your mind halfway through.

Keep your initial materials and equipment as simple as possible. Whether you are working in paint or doing a drawing, take a good look at the subject, decide what you will probably need and make sure it is at hand. Obviously the clothing and background will dictate to some extent which colors you will need, and if you have to compromise on these, it will be detrimental to the overall result.

You may want to start immediately, working directly on the support without making initial sketches or taking photographs. In this case, you must know in your own mind what sort of composition you want and be fairly confident about your general approach. Some aspects of the portrait can only be resolved once you have begun. Tones and colors cannot generally be planned in advance — they will relate to each other in the picture and will be determined as the image develops by what is already established on the canvas or paper.

Composition is all-important when planning your portrait. Even when your subject is a comparatively uncomplicated one, such as the seated figure *opposite*, you must decide whether to use your canvas vertically and how much of the figure to include in the composition.

THE COMPOSITION

Composition in portraiture is often sadly neglected. This is because it is not immediately obvious why a portrait — which is, after all, often no more than a head and shoulders placed in a rectangular shape — should need "composing" at all. And this is a pity because it is precisely the simplicity of the subject which makes it so important to give as much thought as possible to its presentation.

Even if you intend your portrait to be a full-frontal view of a head and shoulders, placed against the plainest possible background, you should still consider the composition. For instance, if there is too much empty space around the subject, this can sometimes look monotonous; if you leave too little background area, your portrait might well seem cramped. Do you want a symmetrical picture, with the figure centered? Or would you prefer to place the subject to one side for a more unusual effect? All these possibilities should be considered at the outset. There is always a choice, and it rarely pays to make the obvious one without first considering the alternatives.

If you were painting a landscape or a still life, you would probably try to create a harmonious arrangement within the picture, avoiding anything which looked discordant, out of place or disruptive. It is generally unwise to lead the eye out of the picture, and a successful composition is usually one which retains the viewer's attention instead of diverting it.

Creating harmony within the picture is less of a problem with a portrait than with other subjects because the human face is a natural focal point. Even so, it is possible to spoil this by clumsy handling. A figure placed too close to the edge of a picture and looking outward past the frame can destroy compositional harmony. A clumsily placed hand or arm can also be an uncomfortable, discordant element.

Double and group portraits are usually arranged so that all the subjects are equally important in the composition. This can be an elaborate arrangement against a complex backdrop, as in *Mr and Mrs Robert Andrews*, the famous conversation piece by Thomas Gainsborough (1727-88). Or the composition might be simple, a grouping of heads against a plain background, such as *The Artist's Servants* by William Hogarth (1697-1764).

There is a fine distinction between a portrait with a background of trees and hills and a landscape that happens to contain a face or figure. The difference is one of emphasis. This is sometimes merely a question of scale — in a portrait, the figure can dominate because of its size and the proportion of picture surface which it fills. Or the definition may be more to do with how the different components are treated. If the face is painted in sharp detail and the background scenery sketchily depicted, then you have a "portrait," however small the subject might be.

SKETCHES

The role of preliminary sketches is twofold. Their main purpose is to work out certain aspects of the portrait before starting the final work. Sketches can also be a valuable reference to be used in the absence of the actual subject. Some artists work entirely from drawings and sketches, needing only one short session with their subject to equip themselves with enough information to enable them to complete the work.

To a certain extent, finding a successful composition is a matter of trial and error. It may be necessary to try several possibilities before arriving at the right one. Small drawings, sometimes called thumbnail sketches, are a useful device. Make a number of these, trying out various arrangements and different ways of composing your subject. Each drawing may take only a few seconds and will help you to work out a satisfactory composition for the final portrait. Possibly you will want to take elements from different drawings, preferring the position of the hands in one, the type of chair in another, the angle of the head in a third, and so on.

Sketches can also help you to decide what scale your subject should be. A larger drawing may also be useful here. Make a rough sketch of the subject, allowing plenty of space all around. Take a piece of cardboard and cut a hole of the same proportions as your support and use this as a viewfinder. By moving the window around on the drawing you will be able to see the best position for your subject. Try windows of various sizes and shapes to help you decide how much background to include and what shaped support would be best for the purpose.

Many artists make elaborate sketches. Some even produce so-called "sketches" in color which are almost indistinguishable from the finished painting, differing

Most portrait artists work from a reference at some stage during a painting. Many make preparatory black and white drawings, *far left*, or quick color sketches *left*. Others rely on photographic reference *above*.

only in the amount of detail and blended finish which is included in the final picture. Such sketches are done relatively quickly, sometimes when the subject is too busy to give a series of lengthy sittings.

PHOTOGRAPHS
Photography should never be used as a substitute for observation and creative thinking, but its value to portrait painters can be enormous. In the past, a rather purist attitude has prevented many artists from using photographs in a constructive and helpful way. Nowadays most artists realize the value of a camera, particularly a Polaroid one, in the field of portraiture.

A Polaroid camera can be used instead of the sketchbook when deciding on a suitable pose or looking for the best lighting effects. The camera is also better able to capture fleeting expressions than the time-consuming process of drawing and painting. This is one of the reasons why

many old portraits tend to look stiff and expressionless — the sitter could not maintain a lively look throughout long, exhausting sittings. Today's artists can capture the gesture of a split second in a photograph, then take as many hours as necessary to translate this onto the canvas.

With good reference photographs to help, the portrait painter can work for long periods without needing the sitter to be there at all. Certainly the clothing, background and much of the rest of the picture can often be done directly from photographs.

But despite its great advantages for the artist, photography has definite limitations and should always be used as a tool rather than as an end in itself — your real concern being with creating a living image of the subject. One of the disadvantages of photography is its tendency to distort. It is now so much part of our lives that we usually believe what we see in photographs, without realizing that our eyes are actually much more sensitive and accurate than the camera lens. The photographed face can be subtly distorted, perhaps with an enlarged nose, or a too-wide or too-narrow face. The experienced portrait painter, trained to observe, sees and corrects these discrepancies. Always believe your own eyes, and check to see whether your camera is actually telling the truth.

Your camera has another shortcoming. It is not selective. Depending on the lens, the camera will normally give you a photograph with the details on any one plane uniformly recorded. The task of deciding what to emphasize and what to leave out is yours.

GETTING A LIKENESS
The ability to "get a good likeness" is often thought of as something beyond the mere technical skill of the artist, a sort of heaven-sent gift which exists independently of artistic talent and which has more to do with some mysterious insight into the character of the subject than with being able to draw or paint a face.

Portrait painters are usually the first to refute this. Although a good likeness is not entirely a question of correct proportions, technical ability and experience have much to do with it. Obviously it is helpful to be able to pinpoint special characteristics and to know the idiosyncratic gestures peculiar to your subject, but the actual "likeness" is something which emerges naturally, an indirect result of close observation and your ability to paint what you see.

SKIN
A common error when mixing flesh tones is to assume we know what color skin is. When painting white people, school children are taught to mix white and red with a little yellow to make it look "real"; black people are usually colored a standard brown, often with exaggerated highlights; oriental faces are quite frequently portrayed as flat yellow shapes. As children we also "know" that the sky is blue, clouds are white, and grass is green.

Such preconceptions are difficult to overcome. For the artist it means close observation and hard work. If we look carefully at the work of most landscape artists, we see that the grass is painted in a whole range of tones and colors, and the sky often contains little or no blue. In many of the landscapes of the English painter John Constable (1776-1837), yellows, browns, blacks, blues and reds are dominant colors in the "green" grass and trees.

In the same way, the portrait artist must learn to look at the subject through fresh eyes. Local color is important, but it should not be taken for granted. Shadows and highlights must be carefully analyzed and should never be simply a darkened or lightened version of the general color. Every shadow and highlight has its own color which will be affected by the reflection of surrounding colors.

Flesh tones are a subtle mix of light and dark, and warm and cool. All portrait painters use green or blue, sometimes both, for the elusive cool shadow tones present in all skin types. In the illustrated demonstrations in the later chapters of this book you will see how different artists approach the problem.

In his *Portrait of André Derain,* Matisse takes a refreshingly new look at the variety of colors in his subject's face, breaking down the planes of light and shade into well-defined areas of coolness and warmth. The shadows are emphatic, depicted in strong purples and greens; the rich warm planes on the illuminated side of the face are depicted in bright reds, oranges and pinks. The loose, textural brushwork in no way detracts from the "likeness." Instead, Matisse has used the rugged finish to emphasize the character and mood of the pose in an individual and perceptive way.

Painters of the Renaissance often gave areas of flesh a coat of terre verte undercoat which was allowed to show through the skin tones, lending a cool glow to the shadow areas. This technique is still employed by some artists, and is particularly effective when acrylic is used as an underpainting. The acrylic dries quickly, enabling layers of thin, transparent color to be built up over the cool base color. The method is described in more detail in Chapter 7.

Although the solid bone structure of the head and face is covered with a disguising layer of flesh and skin, this should not be your major preoccupation in the initial stages, nor should it prevent you from seeing the more important underlying structure. It is a common mistake to overwork the skin in an effort to reproduce its smooth texture and subtly blended planes. When this happens, the face quickly becomes flat and dead. Avoid this by constantly standing back from your work and by treating the skin tones in broad, general terms, using a large brush if you are doing a painting. Superficial characteristics, such as patches of local color, wrinkles and cushions of soft flesh can be helpful when describing form and volume, but they

PAINTING FLESH

There is no easy formula for painting flesh tones. Every artist develops a personal technique, and no two artists approach the subject in exactly the same way. Duccio (active 1278-1319) and many other early Renaissance artists, underpainted all flesh areas in green earth mixed with lead white. In *The Virgin and Child* (detail), *right*, you can see how Duccio allowed the greenish undercoat to show through to represent the cool shadows.

Madame Moitessier Seated (detail), *below left,* by Ingres (1780-1867) shows a subtle, highly finished painting, with the muted cools and warms blended to form realistically smooth flesh. Paul Cézanne (1829-1906) used broken color and strong directional brushstrokes to depict areas of shade, highlight, and local color in his *Self-portrait* (detail) *below right.*

can also be a hindrance if you become obsessively concerned with these to the detriment of the rest of the portrait.

HANDS

Hands are important. If you are going to include them in the portrait, their position and treatment should be carefully considered. Hands can make an image seem alive, giving a feeling of movement to the pose, or they can create an informal atmosphere if they are held in a natural and relaxed way. They are, however, a focal point in the picture, and if they are badly done, there is little chance of their being overlooked.

Unless your portrait is a formal one, perhaps with the subject's hands resting on a table or desk, try to avoid putting both hands on the same level. Hands and face stand out because they are the same tone and color, and it is all too easy to create an uncomfortable pyramid effect with the head as the top of the triangle and the hands as the base. Instead, try to use the similar tones of these features to advantage, arranging the hands to complement the face and to create a harmonious balance in the composition.

Many portrait artists have developed the technique of positioning of the hands to a fine degree. The figures in the portraits of Gwen John (1876-1939), almost without exception, sit with their hands together on their laps. There is nothing jarring or surprising in the composition, and the perfect relationship between the hands and face creates an atmosphere of peace and quiet intimacy.

It is almost always a bad idea to allow part of the hands or fingers to go off the bottom of the picture. The eye is immediately directed to this cut-off point and the bottom edge of the picture becomes unduly important, holding the viewer's attention when it should be concentrating on the face and the rest of the painting. For the same reason, bare arms should not be taken beyond the edge of the composition.

Hands are not as difficult as they might appear, although it often pays to practice by making some studies of your own hands. A common mistake is to attempt to draw or paint each finger separately without regard for the hand as a whole. The result invariably resembles a bunch of sausages, but if you can first establish the planes across the hand, knuckles and wrist — the fingers follow on naturally.

It is not unusual for hands to be sketchily treated in portraits; even in the most finished and detailed of paintings they may be represented by no more than a few well-placed brushstrokes. One reason for doing this is to prevent the hands from competing with the face. We have already noted that hands tend to draw attention, and this is especially true when every finger, knuckle and nail is rendered in minute detail — particularly if they are in the foreground of the composition. It is surprising how minimally drawn and painted hands can actually be without losing either their structure or their credibility.

CLOTHING

You and your subject will possibly have different ideas about which clothes should be worn for the portrait. Sitters may want to wear something in keeping with their image of themselves, a sweater or shirt which has special associations, or a garment that they consider suits them particularly well. You, the artist, will be looking for effects of tone and color, for textural contrast, and for the overall shape as it will look in the composition.

The painter who likes bright colors and patterns may be dismayed if the subject insists on wearing plain gray, but in this case a striking and contrasting background can often solve the problem. Usually a compromise is not hard to find, and serious disagreements are rare.

Nor should drawing and painting fabrics present any real problem. As with skin, it is a mistake to overwork the clothes, which are usually best treated in broad terms in the early stages. Clothes should be developed as part of the whole image, and should generally not be allowed to become more explicit than other elements in the picture.

Different fabrics call for different treatments. Artists of the past have perfected the depiction of lace, velvet, brocade and other richly textured materials to an amazing degree. The Elizabethans, with their jeweled and extravagant costumes, are prime examples of this. Many North European painters of the seventeenth century, notably Frans Hals (1581/5-1666), were also expert in this field. In *The Laughing Cavalier, The Nurse and Child* and many other portraits, Hals painted lace and embroidery almost to a formula. Beautiful stitching is shown in masterly detail, and the decorative needlework on the cavalier's sleeve alone must have taken many hours of patient rendering.

Whatever the texture of the fabric, its shape is almost

HANDS

The position of the hands plays an important role in a portrait. Gwen John (1876-1939) deliberately used hands to create a feeling of harmony in her paintings — in *Girl in a Green Dress, above,* the sitter's hands are placed restfully on her lap. The three photographs, *right,* demonstrate how the position of the model's hands affects both the mood and composition of the portrait.

PAINTING CLOTHING
The Laughing Cavalier by Frans Hals (1581/5-1666), *far left,* shows how important clothing and fabric can be to a portrait. Elaborate lace, *above left,* is painted to the artist's well-practiced formula with the delicate pattern worked in painstaking layers. The motifs embroidered on the cavalier's sleeve are symbolic, and Hals has faithfully rendered every stitch of Cupid's bow, bees, and flames — all emblems of love at that time, *below left.*

always dictated by what is underneath. This is true of all but very stiff or heavily gathered fabrics. Softer ones, such as satin and thin cottons, generally reveal the contours and volumes of the underlying form, and textiles with a surface pattern are often helpful in describing form.

A popular exercise with art teachers is to drape an object – this may be a plaster figure, a simple form or even a live model — for the students to draw. The objective is to draw this in a structural way, using the folds and creases of the cloth to indicate what is underneath. The abstract nature of this exercise makes it imperative to concentrate on the underlying forms, without which the drawing would be nonsensical. For portrait painters there is always a danger-ous and unconscious temptation to rely on recognizable elements, such as the head and hands, to tell the viewer that a body lies beneath the clothes.

THE EYES AND MOUTH

Inexperienced portrait painters frequently overestimate the importance of the eyes. Although they are the natural focal point of the face, it is a mistake to devote a dispropor-tionate amount of time to the eyes — especially in the early stages of the painting. In fact, when any feature is given too

much attention, that part often threatens the unity of the face as a whole.

Remember that the eyelid naturally covers the top part of the iris. A mistake often made by amateurs is to allow the white to show all round the iris, giving the eyes an ab-normal stare. Notice too that the whites of the eyes vary more than is commonly supposed, from very bright to extremely dark. It will help your picture if you establish the tone of these "white" areas correctly. You will probably be surprised at the difference in tone between the eye on the shady side of the head and that on the illuminated side.

It is essential to treat the eyes as structures, not as super-ficial details. Bear in mind that the eye is part of the eyeball, which lies in a socket and which is protected by an upper and lower lid. Depending on the direction of the light, the lid casts a shadow onto the eyeball itself.

When painting or drawing the mouth, always place it in the context of the entire lower part of the face. As we have already seen, the muscles around the lips raise the whole mouth off the surface of the face. The shape of these muscles can be seen as distinct areas of light and shade, so do not be tempted to portray the mouth and lips as flat shapes and painted in one color only.

EYES

It is a common mistake to overwork the eyes. They should always be looked at in the context of the rest of the painting — the close-ups, *left*, are taken from demonstrations in this book and show how the artist tackles the problem of painting the eyes in both oils and watercolor.

MOUTHS

Always look at the mouth in the context of the lower half of the face. It is not a flat shape, but is raised from the face by the underlying muscles. The two close-ups, *left*, are in oil and pastel respectively.

HAIR

Treat hair as a solid mass, looking for planes of light and shade. In the details, *left*, both the painter and the watercolor artist simplify the forms within the hair into broad areas of dark and light.

HAIR

Hair, especially thick hair, can often obscure the shape of the scalp and the structure of the head. This makes it easy to overlook the fact that the hair grows from the scalp and that the shape of the hair is dictated partly by the shape of the head underneath. The line where the hair starts and the face stops is a superficial one.

The most striking thing about hair is its texture. We see the thousands of individual hairs which make up the whole and we wonder how it can possibly be interpreted in a drawing or painting.

Most artists treat the hair as a solid mass, looking for planes of light and shade within the overall shape. Texture is sometimes introduced into this established form, although many painters prefer to leave the hair in a comparatively simplified state. Even in some of the portraits by Frans Hals and Rembrandt, where the hair looks extremely realistic, it has first been established in similar, solid masses.

THE SELF-PORTRAIT

The great advantage of the self-portrait is that you are your own model and are therefore inexpensive, reliable and available at times that suit you. Approach the work just as you would any other subject, making sure that you are comfortable and have a good view of yourself in the mirror. Above all do not neglect to mark the position of the easel, the mirror and your feet so that when you come back to the painting you will be able to take up your position again.

Strangely, it is usually difficult to "see" ourselves properly. Most of us have special expressions which we reserve for the mirror, and which friends insist are nothing like our real selves. The same thing happens with the self-portrait, and the pose you select can be stiff and odd-looking, so try to relax and to forget who the subject is.

It is also true that human eyesight is not perfect. Many people have slight astigmatism which only becomes noticeable when they look at one of their portraits — especially a self-portrait — in a mirror. The reflected image often reveals a slightly distorted face — possibly bulging at one side, unevenly placed eyes, and many other irregularities which were not noticeable before. This eyesight deficiency has long been recognized by portrait painters, and the "mirror test" is a common method of checking the slight distortions it can cause.

CHAPTER SIX

OIL

Oil paints are the traditional medium for portrait painting, and when we talk of the history of portraiture what we really mean is the history of painting portraits in oil. The early fifteenth-century Dutch painter, Jan van Eyck, popularly credited with the invention of oil paint, was also a major figure in the field of portrait painting. Most portraits done since that time are oil paintings, and even today, when artists are experimenting with an ever-increasing range of new materials, the majority of professional portrait painters work in oil.

There are two basic approaches to using oil paint. The traditional method is first to draw the image on to the support and then to apply a monochrome underpainting before painting the main color. This approach, often referred to as "classical" painting, allows the tonal composition to be worked out before any color is added. By separating the stages in this way, many artists find the whole painting process is made considerably easier, because it enables them to concentrate on one element of the picture at a time.

The alternative, or "direct" approach (also called alla prima painting) involves working directly onto the support with the minimum of drawing or preliminary sketching. This method relies on freshness of color and a lively or textured picture surface. The painting should not be overworked, and it is often better to work quickly, producing several paintings in rapid succession rather than making laborious corrections which can destroy the very qualities which the "direct" method sets out to achieve.

CORNER KEY

STRETCHER

PLYWOOD

Materials

The essentials of oil painting are a selection of paints, some brushes, a palette, turpentine or mineral spirit and a surface to paint on. This surface, or support, can be primed canvas, or it can be a less expensive alternative like masonite. Other items, such as painting knives and palette knives, can be added to these basics as you become better acquainted with the medium and, hence, with your particular needs.

Supports
Oils are traditionally done on prepared canvas, although wood, masonite, cardboard and paper are all suitable, provided they have been properly prepared. Primed canvas, canvas boards and pads or sheets of specially prepared oil paper are available from artists' suppliers, ready for immediate use. Alternatively, you can prepare your own supports, which is by far the cheapest method. In this way you have absolute control over the proportions and texture, and can build up a stock of relatively inexpensive supports to practice on.

Stretching your own canvases is easy once you know how. There are various fabrics to choose from, the best being pure linen, because it stretches well and provides a taut, receptive surface to paint on. Cheaper alternatives are cotton, linen crash and a mixture of linen and cotton. The wooden stretchers can be bought in different lengths and are easily slotted together to make rectangles of any size and proportion.

HARDBOARD:
ROUGH SIDE

PALETTE KNIVES AND PAINTING KNIVES

HARDBOARD: SMOOTH SIDE

To stretch your own canvas, assemble the frame by fitting the four wooden stretcher pieces together. Cut your fabric slightly larger than this frame — about 3in all around should be ample. Place the fabric on the floor and lay the frame over this. The wooden supports are usually beveled along one side to prevent a sharp edge from showing on the canvas. This beveled edge goes along the inside of the frame. Starting with one of the longest sides, fold the fabric over and staple or tack it to the back of the stretcher. Repeat this on the opposite side of the canvas. Continue fixing the fabric to the frame in this way, starting from one of these central points and working toward the corner. Repeat this on the opposite section, and continue in this way until all the sides are firmly fixed.

Whether you use canvas or another fabric, it must be sized and primed before use or the paint will simply sink into it. Sizing also protects the canvas from the long-term rotting effects of the paint and primer. Size — or animal-skin glue, if you are using this — usually comes in crystal form. This is dissolved in water over heat, then brushed onto the fabric while still warm. The fabric tautens as the size dries. When the size is dry, apply a coat of ground or canvas primer to the canvas. This seals the fabric and provides a good surface to paint on. You can buy grounds in artists' suppliers. An alternative, used successfully by many artists, is ordinary waterbased house paint.

Acrylic primers are fine for use with oils, but oil primers must not be used for acrylics. Many commercially prepared surfaces are now suitable for both, but check carefully, because acrylic paint eventually comes away from an oily support — a point to bear in mind if you use an acrylic underpainting to start an oil painting.

OIL PRIMER

CANVAS BOARDS

OIL SKETCHING PAPER

WIN GEL

LINSEED OIL

MINERAL SPIRIT

METAL DIPPER

Masonite, cardboard and paper are good, cheap alternatives to stretched canvas. These can be cut to any size, but must also be treated with size and primer or undercoat before use. You can prevent a large piece of masonite from warping by screwing or nailing two wooden battens to the back, but take care that the screws or nails do not come through.

Paints

Oil paints are sold in tubes and are available in two grades, artists' and students'. Artists' colors, as the name implies, are better quality, and this is reflected in the price. Beginners often start off with the cheaper variety, gradually changing to the better grade as they become more proficient in the medium. Some pigments used in the manufacture of paint are less permanent than others. These tend to fade when exposed to light or when mixed with other colors. Tubes of paint are usually graded – the more permanent colors being the most expensive. If possible, try to avoid the more "fugitive" colors altogether.

Oil media

Oil paint is made from pigment mixed with a binder, such as poppy-seed oil or linseed oil. Colour can be used thickly, direct from the tube, or it can be diluted with turpentine or mineral spirit in the same way that watercolor is diluted with water. Genuine turpentine is the best diluent, although the cheaper mineral spirit, or turpentine substitute, is often used instead.

Used on its own, turpentine produces a mat finish and considerably accelerates the drying time of the paint. However, the paint surface can become dull and lifeless if too much turpentine is used, and for this reason it is generally used in conjunction with an oil medium which lends texture and body to the paint. The

PLASTIC DIPPER

HOG HAIR FILBERT No.6

HOG HAIR ROUND No.8

HOG HAIR BRIGHT No.7

WOODEN PALETTE

PAPER PALETTE

ARTIST'S OIL COLORS

most common of these substances is linseed oil. This is usually mixed with the turpentine in a ratio of approximately 60:40. For a thicker consistency, which dries more quickly, you can add a little varnish to the linseed and turpentine.

Brushes

Aim for a selection of good-quality brushes. The stiff ones are made from hog hair, softer ones from sable or squirrel. An increasing selection of synthetic brushes is now available in both the stiffer and softer varieties. Synthetic brushes are usually considerably cheaper than natural bristles.

Brushes come in a variety of shapes. The basic ones are round, bright, filbert and flat. Brights and flats are similar, but flats have longer bristles and are especially good for long, tapering strokes; rounds are good, general-purpose brushes, and a wide range of sizes of this type is useful. Filberts are flattened with slightly rounded ends to produce more controlled strokes.

Apart from these standard shapes, there are several "specialist" brushes which can be used to obtain a variety of effects. Of these, the fan brush is probably the most common.

Palettes

Oil-painting palettes are traditionally made of wood. These come in a range of sizes and should be treated with linseed oil before use. Disposable palettes are also available.

Painting and palette knives

Palette knives are long and flexible, and can be used for cleaning the palette and mixing paint as well as applying it to the painting. Painting knives are specifically designed for laying paint on the support, usually to achieve a thickly impastoed effect.

SYNTHETIC BRIGHT No.14

SYNTHETIC FAN-SHAPED
BLENDER No.6

SABLE BRIGHT No.8

SABLE ROUND No.4

Anita in Miniature

To reduce this strong and colorful subject to a miniature portrait was something of an experiment for the artist. She normally works slowly on a much larger scale, and here she was required to produce a tiny portrait comparatively quickly.

This artist works in a bright color key, relating a set of strong, bright tones to each other. She lays these separately on the canvas, placing pure colors side by side. The boldness of this approach has given an intense and almost jewellike appearance to this miniature. Color was applied very locally, in small blocks, and then blended with a sable brush to form a continuous plane.

For a palette, the artist used a piece of cardboard, which absorbed some of the oil from the paints, helping the colors to dry faster between applications and therefore speeding up the whole process. This artist prefers a mat finish, and getting rid of some of the oil also helped her to achieve this.

Sable brushes — mostly usually used for watercolors — enabled the artist to paint in the tiny, intricate strokes necessary for a miniature. She managed to translate her normal bold style into the smaller format, bringing out the bright earthiness of the girl's headgear and the glow of her skin.

1 Anita, *right,* frequently models for the artist. Usually the paintings are large, and this miniature is something of an experiment.

2 A preliminary pencil drawing establishes the position of the head and shoulders on the rectangular support. The features are drawn accurately at this stage *below.* The pencil line is then rubbed down with a cloth to remove excess graphite and dust which might mix with the paint and distort the colors.

3 Using yellow ocher, alizarin crimson, titanium white, violet, terre verte, ultramarine, cobalt blue, Naples yellow, and cerulean blue, the artist begins to block in the flesh tones *left*. All the flesh tints are mixed from these basic colors. The artist refers to the subject constantly as she works, exaggerating both the local and reflected colors found in the face. Each plane is clearly defined, and the colors and tones are treated as separate elements of the whole face. Black is used only to represent a local color — it is never used to tone down a bright color. The artist always works directly on a white support without any underpainting. White shows through the paint, creating a range of bright, luminous colors across the picture surface.

4 A small area of light blue is established behind the subject. This is an approximate color of the eventual background and helps the artist to mix the correct flesh tones by relating them to a background tone. Here the artist applies cool dark tones to the shaded parts of the neck *above*.

5 The form of the face emerges as the planes of light and shade are established. A narrow strip of cold reflected light down the shaded side of the face prevents that side of the head from merging into the blue background *above*.

47

6 At this stage the artist completes the light blue background, taking this right up to the outline of the subject with a No. 8 sable brush *above*. The flat blue is a simplified version of the real background, which the artist considers too complex for a small portrait.

7 The painting so far shows the partially established facial tones against the final background *right*. To offset the distorting effect of unpainted white canvas, the artist breaks up these areas with dabs of tone and local color.

8 Working across the painting, the artist blocks in pale warm flesh tones on the light side of the neck. The warm tones are mixed mainly from red, yellow ocher and white. Cool areas are generally painted in green-blue or purple-red. Here, *right*, the light flesh tones are taken up to the background and, because the paint is used fairly thickly, the color is opaque enough to cover the edge of the blue and produce a sharp outline.

9 Rowney rose is lightened with white to make the basic bright pink of Anita's blouse. Initially this is applied as a solid flat shape, *left,* the color picking out the warm pinks of the face. Again, the thick opaque paint is taken up to and over the flesh color to form a sharp edge.

10 A touch of alizarin crimson is blended with the bright pink to suggest the rounded form of the shoulders *above.*

CHOOSING A COLOR KEY

Some artists choose a low color key, working from a range of subdued hues. Others prefer brighter colors, or a high color key. The choice is a personal one, the important thing being how the colors relate to each other in the picture.

Here the artist uses comparatively bright colors. The initial blocking-in is done in fairly vivid tones, the blues, reds and greens being quite discernible in the overall image. This blocking-in sets the "key" for the rest of the painting, and the subtle tones and planes of the face are well observed in a range of distinct, clear colors.

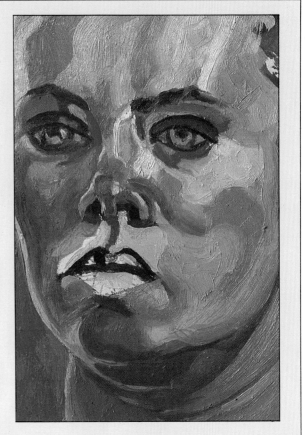

11 Moving back to the face, the artist continues to block in the flesh tones *right*. The bright pink around the eye reflects the Rowney rose and white of the blouse.

12 All the general skin tones are now complete *below*. The round form of the neck and the volumes within the head and face can be seen clearly, created from a systematic filling in of flat shapes.

13 Exaggerating the brightness of the real colors, the artist paints in the patterned scarf *right*. Each of these colors is a key color in the various flesh mixtures, and the vividly depicted headscarf has a "lifting" effect on the whole portrait by bringing out and heightening the important skin colors.

What the artist used

The small hardboard support measuring approximately 6in×5in was cut from a larger sheet of Masonite and treated with oil primer. A selection of round sable brushes, Nos. 2, 3, 5 and 8, was used to apply the oil color which was mixed with turpentine. The artist worked from a palette of titanium white, yellow ocher, alizarin crimson, voilet, terre verte, cobalt blue, ultramarine, cerulean blue, Naples yellow, cadmium yellow, cadmium red, and Rowney rose. A B pencil was used for the preliminary drawing.

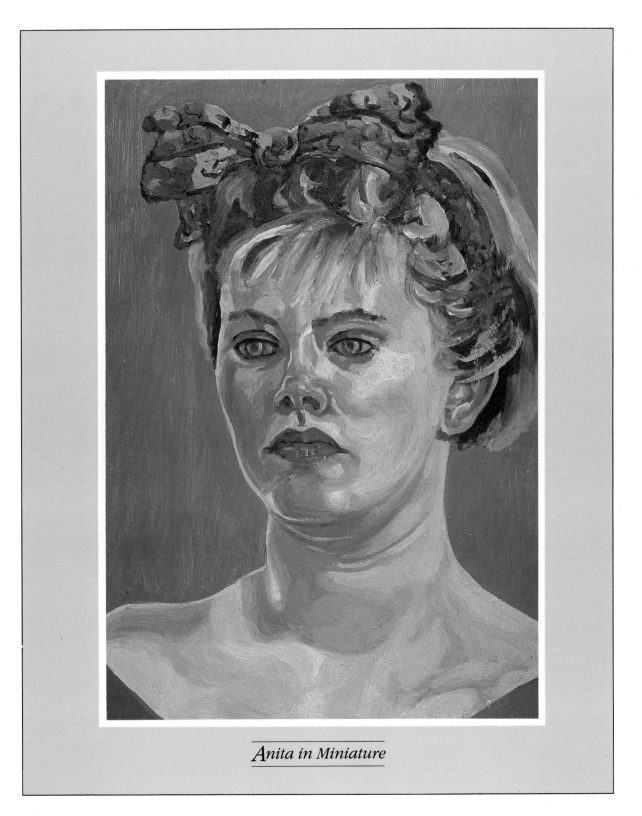

Anita in Miniature

Girl in a Yellow T-shirt

This portrait has been composed in a straightforward, simple way, using a lot of plain space, with the figure low down in the picture. There is nothing to distract attention from the expressive face and the strikingly bright shirt.

At an earlier stage in the painting, the artist put in a shadow, giving a specific space between the figure and the background. This gave the background reality as a surface, making it appear as a wall or board. However, the artist then decided to concentrate instead on the graphic qualities of the figure, and removed the shadow. This made the background change, so that it has ceased to exist in space, becoming flat, with nothing to indicate any dimension. The three-dimensional qualities of the picture are provided by the well-observed, sculpted form of the figure.

The portrait takes a full-frontal, completely symmetrical view of its subject. This simple approach has been made to look slightly out of the ordinary by placing the figure well down in the picture. Exactly the same margin of space around the figure might have been monotonous, but the lower position of the subject has created an airiness, emphasizing the carefree, youthful and fresh look of the whole portrait.

One of the most interesting tasks in this portrait was to capture the variety of tones and colors in the girl's face. The local facial color of people of different races can be very different, but light and shade largely determine the tone — just as they do with anything else. For both dark-skinned and light-skinned people, the local color must determine the basic tone to some degree, but it is the strength and direction of the light falling on the facial planes which really create the final color variations.

The artist has drawn out the shapes of the tonal planes in pencil, and has filled them in as areas of flat color. On the face, for instance, the artist mixed several tones of each color required, then looked carefully to relate them to each other. The slow-drying quality of oil paint enabled these to be blended together to give the impression of soft, rounded form.

1 The artist liked the strikingly graphic qualities of this woman in bright yellow against the plain gray wall *right*.

2 The outline of the subject is drawn with a well-sharpened F pencil, indicating the areas of light and shade *right*. The drawing is kept deliberately simple to act as a guide in the initial painting stages.

3 *Above,* the hair is painted in a mixture of black, raw umber, and cobalt blue, with a No. 4 round synthetic brush. Then the contours of the face are established in brown. Unlike many painters, this artist does not begin by establishing the general areas of skin tone, working over the whole face until the tones are correct in relation to each other. He prefers to work systematically, starting in one place and filling in the image piece by piece, rather like a jigsaw puzzle. By carefully painting each area of tone or color correctly in relation to its neighbor, he causes the subject to emerge gradually as the "filling in" progresses.

4 With a basic mixture of burnt sienna, cadmium red, cobalt blue, and chrome orange, the artist starts to block in the skin tones *above.* By working from the top down, he avoids smudging the wet paint.

5 The completed face, *left,* shows a range of tones obtained from the basic mixture. The planes of light and shade meet and overlap in carefully observed, natural shapes.

SKIN TONES

This artist prefers to work from the top of the head downward to avoid smudging the work already done. The skin tones here are built up patch by patch, rather like a jigsaw puzzle, each one being carefully related to those already established. Occasionally the artist goes back over the work, changing or modifying particular areas.

Black skin is more affected by reflected light than white skin, and the artist has used these strong planes of light to describe the form and contours of the face.

6 Using cerulean blue, titanium white and black, the artist starts to block in the background *above*. Color is applied as evenly as possible with a No. 8 flat bristle brush. A No. 3 sable brush is used to take the color up to the outline of the subject — care being taken to preserve the irregular, complex shape of the hairline and the contours of the face and shoulders.

7 Cadmium yellow, titanium white, yellow ocher and a little black are used for the T-shirt *above*. The shadows are indicated in gray.

8 A darker background color is used for the bold shadow *right*. The artist decides that this spoils the simplicity of the composition, and completes the portrait by removing the heavy shadow and by brightening the color of the girl's T-shirt.

Girl in a Yellow T-shirt

What the artist used

For this portrait in oils the artist chose to work on stretched Herston flax canvas. This was pre-primed for oil paint. He worked from a palette of titanium white, burnt sienna, cadmium red, chrome orange, cobalt blue, ivory black, raw umber, cerulean blue, cadmium yellow and yellow ocher. The paint was mixed with Rowney's Alkyd Medium. For the background and other large areas, the artist blocked in the color with a No. 8 flat bristle brush. Other brushes used were a No. 6 flat; a No. 4 synthetic round; and sable brushes, Nos. 2 and 3. The preliminary drawing was done with an F pencil.

Girl in Profile

The girl's profile, standing out strongly against a dark flat background, provides the opportunity for the use of space as a "negative shape." The artist has done this deliberately, by cutting off the top and the back of the head, resulting in two interlocking shapes — the head and the space into which it faces.

A straight profile against a flat gray background runs the risk of becoming a rather boring picture, but the artist has avoided this by paying detailed attention to the interplay of the main shapes. The hair forms a definite shape, and the negative shape, opposite the face, is an important part of the composition. If you could forget that a face is represented here, the division of the space would work well as an abstract. For instance, before the face was fully painted in, you could imagine the picture as two abstract shapes separated by a taut and disciplined dividing line, and your attention could be flicked from one shape to the other, treating each one in turn as the subject and the other as the background.

The artist has used glazing to build up the flesh tones in the face, avoiding wedges of opaque color for different patches of light and shade. Flesh does not consist of a patchwork of tones and colors — it is much more subtle than that. From a visual point of view, it is made up of overlapping veils of translucent color. By using glazing, a natural transition from light to dark, from cool to warm, or vice versa, becomes technically possible.

1 The composition of this profile portrait, *right,* is based on the interlocking shapes of the girl's face and the negative background space.

2 Using a thin wash of turpentine and burnt umber, the artist blocks in the shadow areas of the hair and face *right.* The larger background area is painted with a No. 4 flat bristle brush; the more intricate facial features are added with a No. 2 flat bristle brush. By establishing the main areas in the early stages, the artist is able to gradually introduce color into the painting without worrying too much about tonal contrast and depth. The color is applied thinly to allow transparent glazes of color to be built up gradually.

3 Using a mixture of cadmium red, burnt umber and white, the artist loosely blocks in the warm facial tones with the No. 4 brush *left*. The light hair color is yellow ocher and white.

4 The shadows around the eyes are painted with black, white, and a touch of burnt umber *below*. The artist uses the No. 2 brush to obtain the tiny precise areas of varying tones.

5 The artist works into the skin tones, developing the planes of light and shade *below*. Each small area of warm highlight and cool shadow is carefully applied in thin layers as the artist constantly refers to the subject.

6 Ultramarine and black are mixed together and applied to the background area. The artist uses a large brush to obtain a flat, even expanse of color. Delicate strands of hair are added in yellow ocher and white *above*.

What the artist used

The painting was done on a fairly small scale − 12in × 15in − and the artist chose to work on a prepared canvas board. Flat bristle brushes, Nos. 2 and 4, were used to apply the oil paint. The palette consisted of eight colors: black, burnt sienna, burnt umber, cadmium red medium, scarlet lake, ultramarine, white, and yellow ocher. For mixing the thin glazes of color, the artist used turpentine and linseed oil (too much turpentine can spoil a glaze, and the artist kept its use to a minimum).

GLAZING

Glazing is a method of building up color in thin layers, or of applying a transparent layer over a solid one so that the color of the first is slightly changed. The method produces a luminous finish which makes it particularly appropriate for painting the subtle, translucent tones of the skin, but it is a relatively slow process, because each layer must be allowed to dry.

When thinning oil paints for glazing, do not use turpentine alone as a thinner, and never use turpentine substitute. Turpentine is sometimes mixed with linseed oil, but linseed oil is not ideal for glazing, since it tends to move after being laid. Ideally, a proper glazing medium should be used, such as the alkyd medium sold under the name of Liquin. When doing glazes in this way, increase the oil or glazing-medium content with each new layer of color.

Girl in Profile

59

Woman Sleeping

In this close-up portrait of a woman sleeping the composition is particularly interesting and unusual. The woman's head slants diagonally across the picture, yet seems also to fill it, so that the diagonal does not intrude too much.

The artist has faced at least two main tasks: that of depicting the peaceful sleeping pose of the model reclining on a sofa, and that of capturing the tones and shadows of the skin.

The sleeping posture would have been easier to indicate by showing more of the model's body on the sofa; painting only the head made it more difficult. The use of the diagonal has helped to achieve the effect, as the head is placed across the picture in a way that naturally indicates a reclining position.

First, the artist sketched in the outline of the head with willow charcoal to establish the broad form. Charcoal is a good medium for this initial work, because it is rough and immediate, and thus prevents any over-attention to small detail, irrelevant in the early stages. She then quickly worked over the charcoal outline with a B pencil, developing the drawing and making a more specific outline, after which the surface was wiped to remove excess charcoal dust.

The artist blocked in the background around the head and the edge of the headscarf in a black/blue, taking the opportunity to redefine the contours of the head. She then turned her attention to what she noted to be an area of darker skin tone on and just below the uppermost eye. Many portrait painters put in skin tones across the whole face, moving from one area to the other, lightening and darkening certain areas, so that they come up, or tone down, in relation to each other.

Here the approach was different: the artist first developed the uppermost eye in some detail — an area which included some of the very lightest and very darkest tones. Taking these as a guide, she worked outward from this point, relating each new area to those already established.

Throughout the painting the artist looked constantly at the subject, since she not only had to pick out the tiny, irregular planes of light and shade, but also had to consider the local color. For instance, the cheeks have a naturally rosy hue, while the inside corners of the eye cavity have a cooler, darker local color. She was careful, too, not to lose the internal contours — the outline of the nose, eyes and mouth, which were developed in a linear way with a small paintbrush.

1 Although the artist works on such a small scale — this painting measures 8in x 8in — she prefers to use a large, stable easel *right*.

2 The head and features are sketched in charcoal *left*. The artist's prime interest is in the face and flesh tones, so the head is placed prominently, filling the whole picture area.

3 Any excess charcoal dust is wiped off the support *left*. Charcoal dust mixes with all types of paint, usually resulting in dirty, messy colors. Here the artist rubs away almost all the drawing, leaving only a faint outline to act as a guide for the painting.

4 The dark blue background and the lighter toned headscarf are blocked in. The artist then begins to work on the face, starting at the eye and working outward *above*.

5 Planes of light and shade are filled in piece by piece *right*. Each new patch of warm or cool tone is related to the adjoining area and is painted as a flat plane of color.

WARM/COOL SKIN TONES

The human skin is composed of many shades of varying warm and light tones. Generally, in white skins, the shadows have overtones of blue, green or purple, while the lighter areas are mainly yellows, pinks and oranges. However, the division is not absolute. Often there are warmish tones in the shadow areas and comparatively cool tones in the lighter areas and highlights. Much depends on the subject's skin color and the lighting.

A close-up view of this face shows how the artist has carefully observed the changing color temperatures across the surface of the skin, portraying these in accurate and clearly defined planes.

6 A No. 2 sable brush is used for the small shapes of flesh tone *top left*. The image emerges gradually as each patch is filled in.

8 The flesh tones are all mixed from yellow ocher, alizarin crimson, titanium white, cadmium red, violet, terre verte, ultramarine, cobalt blue, cerulean blue, and Naples yellow *above*.

7 Shaded areas are mainly cool, light areas are mainly warm. Here the deep shadows around the nose are painted in a dark, cool purple *left*.

Woman Sleeping

What the artist used

Working on a piece of primed masonite measuring 8in×8in, the artist started by drawing the subject with willow charcoal. She worked from a palette of titanium white, yellow ocher, alizarin, violet, terre verte, ultramarine blue, cobalt blue, cerulean blue, Naples yellow, Rowney rose, Rowney orange, Payne's gray, cadmium yellow and cadmium red. Colors were applied with a selection of round sable brushes, Nos. 2, 3, 4 and 5.

CHAPTER SEVEN

ACRYLIC

The advent of acrylic paints in the early part of this century was the most significant discovery in artists' materials for more than five hundred years. It offered many of the advantages of oil paints with the additional ones of being fast-drying and practically indestructible once applied to the support.

An extraordinarily versatile medium, acrylic is particularly helpful to portrait painters. The traditional technique of building up flesh tones in a series of transparent layers, or glazes, can be achieved in a matter of minutes, and thinned acrylic dries almost immediately, whereas with the slower-drying oil paint, glazing is a lengthy procedure because each layer must dry before the next is applied. Hence warm and cool tones can be applied on top of each other to create the "living" tones of skin without the color looking dead or muddy.

Its quick-drying capacity makes acrylic ideal for underpainting. Artists of the past frequently painted a monochrome version of their subject before introducing color. Using acrylics, such an underpainting can be ready to work on within a few minutes of application. It is also possible to use oil paint over acrylic, and many artists who work mainly in oils find it useful to use acrylics for the initial blocking in.

Acrylic can be applied thickly for rich impastos, or very diluted to obtain transparent washes. But although the results sometimes resemble oil or watercolor, it is a mistake to regard it as a substitute for either. Acrylic is a medium in its own right, very different from any other, and patience and practice are required to get the best results.

MAT VARNISH

GLOSS VARNISH

HARDBOARD:
SMOOTH SIDE

HARDBOARD:
ROUGH SIDE

PLYWOOD

ACRYLIC PRIMER

CRYLA TEXTURE PASTE

ROBESON'S
BRUSHMARK

Materials

Compared with oil and watercolor, acrylic is a very new medium. Its main advantage is that it is harder and more permanent than traditional media. It is also highly resilient and resistant to atmospheric conditions, such as damp and decomposition, and once it is dry, it retains its texture and color.

Supports

Acrylic paints can be used on almost any type of surface. Canvas, masonite and paper are the most popular choices, although there are many more unusual supports which are just as suitable, such as wood, plastic, metal and various fabrics.

It is not necessary to size acrylic supports, but a special acrylic primer available from artists' suppliers is normally used. Under no circumstances should oil grounds and primers be used, and ordinary emulsion grounds are not usually compatible with acrylics.

Commercially prepared surfaces — canvas, boards and paper — are also available, but again you should make sure they have been treated for acrylics and not for oils.

There are several cheaper alternatives to bought surfaces. As with oils, you can use paper, cardboard and canvas, treated with the appropriate acrylic primer. Cheap paper will probably wrinkle if you use the paint diluted, so use a good-quality thick one. You can also stretch your own canvas (see under Materials section in Chapter 6) and give it two or three coats of acrylic primer. Many artists use dilute acrylic directly on raw, unprimed canvas to obtain the luminous wash effect known as "staining."

Paints

Almost every manufacturer of artists' materials now produces its own brand of acrylic paint. These have impressive technical names like dioxazine purple and naphthol crimson – names which reflect their laboratory origins.

The thickness of the paint depends on the brand, but the consistency is generally similar to that of gouache or oils. Rowney make a slightly runnier version in their softly textured "Flow Formula" series. PVA colors are cheaper than acrylics and are made with less costly pigments, although they share the hardwearing and quick-drying advantages. Cheap vinyl colors are sold in larger quantities especially for use on big areas. Alkyds are acrylic-based paints which are mixed with turpentine instead of water.

You are not confined to using acrylics by themselves when working in this medium. Acrylics are particularly good mixers and can be combined effectively with other materials. They are popular for collage work, a method of creating images by gluing various materials or. top of each other. One characteristic of acrylics, which makes them ideal for collages, is their adhesiveness — you can stick a shape or cut-out into wet paint or acrylic medium.

LIQUITEX PAINT

PALETTE KNIVES

It is also possible to achieve highly textured paint surfaces by mixing sand, sawdust and other suitable materials with the paint before applying it to the support.

Brushes

Brushes suitable for oil or watercolor are generally also suitable for acrylics, but you may develop a different way of working, which will call for different brushes. Concentrate on acquiring a workable selection of a few useful shapes and sizes, adding to these gradually as you discover what your specific needs are.

Oil painting brushes are normally made of bristle, whereas the best watercolor brushes are sable. Both types can be used for acrylics, but the bristle brushes, which are stiffer, are generally more appropriate when the paint is applied thickly in the manner normally associated with oil paint. Soft watercolor brushes are usually preferred for more translucent, diluted paint effects.

All brush types are now available in nylon. These are hard-wearing, and many artists find the synthetic brushes particularly compatible with the synthetic acrylic paint. It is easier to remove acrylic paint from nylon brushes, but, like all brushes, they must be cleaned well and frequently, since acrylic paint dries so fast that they can become stiff and unusable very quickly. The large nylon brushes sold in hardware and decorator's stores are excellent for applying large areas of flat color.

SYNTHETIC FAN-SHAPED
BLENDER NO.4

HOG HAIR FLAT NO.8

HOG HAIR ROUND NO.3

Media

Acrylics are not compatible with the media used for oil paint. You can buy various substances which can be mixed with the paint to achieve different effects and, of course, the paints can also be thinned with water. Gloss and mat media – as their names suggest – can be added to make the paint surface dull or shiny, and there is a particularly useful medium called retarder, made of glycerine, which slows down the drying of the paint, thus giving you more time to correct the image, manipulate the paint and adjust the tones.

For creating prominent, textured brushstrokes, use gel medium, which comes in a tube and is thicker than the paint itself. If you want to make your colors really thick, mix the paint with texture or modeling paste. This can be built up on the surface of the support to form a heavy impasto, and is particularly effective when applied with a palette or painting knife.

Other equipment

There is generally little difference between the equipment used with acrylic and that used with oil or watercolor. However, it is better to obtain a white, plastic palette instead of the usual wooden one, because it is easier to clean the hard acrylic paint from a plastic surface.

If you find the quick-drying color hard to handle, there is a special palette which is designed to help, the Rowney "Staywet" palette, which uses the principle of osmosis to keep colors wet for several days. You can also keep the paint wet on your palette by occasionally sprinkling it with water or spraying with an atomizer.

SYNTHETIC BRIGHT NO.6

SYNTHETIC ROUND NO.11

FLOW FORMULA ACRYLIC PAINT

SABLE ROUND NO.8

Melissa, from a Photograph

In this portrait — done entirely from a photograph — of a little girl in a bright colored dress the artist chose to tone down the background, painting it in neutral colors, although a scumbling of lighter color was applied to the background surface to give· an interesting texture. The texture became modified as the artist worked, but still retains a lively surface in the final picture.

The portrait is quite formally composed, the main task being to capture the lively personality of the girl in such a way as to counteract the symmetry and conventionality of the pose.

The artist used acrylic for the background — taking advantage of its quick-drying property — and also for the hair, the basic skin tones and the large blue expanses of the girl's dress. He then developed the more subtle skin tones, some parts of the face, such as the mouth, and the details of the dress, with the slower-drying and more malleable oil paint.

The artist worked from a fairly small-scale photograph, making the drawing stage important. This is the stage at which he interpreted and developed the rather blurred and indistinct tonal variation in the photograph. This was done very clearly, in a hard pencil, and the artist made a definite statement, taking firm decisions about the way the picture was to develop.

Skin tones were mixed on a large piece of white formica, enabling the artist to see clearly what he was using. A large white surface is useful because you can mix a complete set of tones, ranging from very light to very dark, and you can keep these separate, going back to the required color as necessary. Not all artists work in this way. Some prefer to start off with a basic skin tone, modifying this by adding other colors to obtain tonal variation.

The crisp edge on the narrow band of brown which divides the background area was achieved with masking tape. The tape was pressed firmly onto the canvas along the straight edge of the strip, and fairly thick brown paint was used on top of it. (If paint is too thin, it will tend to run under masking tape.)

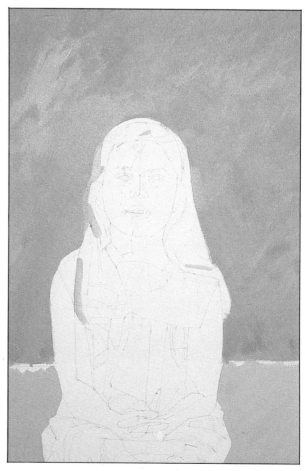

1 This portrait of Melissa, a young friend of the artist, was painted from an informal snapshot *right*.

2 Working on pre-primed canvas, the artist first makes a detailed drawing of the subject using an F pencil. A careful outline is sketched in, and facial features and areas of light and shade are accurately indicated. The figure is placed in the lower half of the rectangular canvas to allow plenty of background space and to offset the rather conventional full-frontal pose. The lighter background area is painted with raw umber, titanium white and Payne's gray; small amounts of ivory black and burnt umber are added for the dark area *right*.

3 With a mixture of ivory black and burnt umber, the artist blocks in the dark areas of the girl's hair *right*. The dark tones are predominantly black; the lighter areas contain more burnt umber. Two brushes are used here – a No. 2 bristle for the broader expanses of color, and a No. 3 sable for the delicate outlines and complex edges. At this stage the lighter tones are left as patches of white canvas. These will be filled in later to tone with the rest of the image as it is developed.

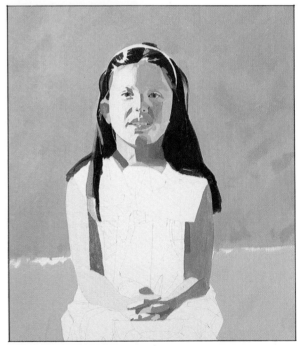

4 Here the artist paints dark and medium flesh tones mixed from varying quantities of cadmium red, yellow ocher, cadmium orange, titanium white and cobalt blue *left*.

5 The general skin tones of the face and arms are now established *above*. Areas of white canvas are left to represent highlights.

6 The basic colors and tones of the dress are painted in a mixture of turquoise, cerulean, Payne's gray and titanium white *right*. The light dress tone is achieved by adding extra white to the basic mixture.

7 The basic overall tones are established in a series of built-up patches of flat acrylic color, *below,* and the artist is now ready to work into the image the more malleable oil paint. Notice how the artist has not, so far, attempted to blend the tiny areas of acrylic color. Instead, they are left to merge "optically," in the viewer's eye.

8 Working with a No. 2 sable brush, the artist builds up the facial details, *above,* referring continually to the photographic reference.

THE MOUTH

The mouth in this portrait is gradually built up from three basic skin tones — light, medium and dark. These are mixed from white, cadmium red, yellow ocher, cadmium orange and cobalt blue, the amount of white determining the actual tone. The artist starts by filling a middle tone, adding the highlights and, finally, the dark shadows.

This method of working depends on accurate drawing for its success. Another artist might take a completely different approach, possibly starting with the broad form of the mouth, and then developing this to create the lips, with the highlights being added last. The most important thing to remember is that the mouth is not a flat shape, and that the lips and the face around the mouth have distinct form and volume.

9 The artist uses masking tape to achieve the straight edges of the brown band along the seat. The tape is carefully removed to avoid smudging the paint *left*. The horizontal brown strip stands out from the pale background, strengthening the composition.

10 Moving from one area to another, the artist continues to develop the tone and detail, improving the form and adding increased depth to the image. Here, *right,* the artist strengthens and blends the contours of the face.

11 Using a No. 3 bristle brush, the artist adds white highlights to the dress *below.* The oil color is brighter than the flat white of the canvas primer, the added contrast giving vibrancy and sparkle to the colored dress. Because the acrylic underpainting is now quite dry, the artist is able to take the oil color over the edge of the blue to make a crisp, clean shape.

12 The close-up, *above,* shows how the skin tones benefit from a combination of flat, acrylic underpainting and final detail, added in oil.

What the artist used

The artist worked on pre-stretched Herston flax canvas, manufactured by Daler. This support measured approximately 22in × 18in. For the acrylic blocking-in, he used a palette of black, titanium white, raw umber, Payne's gray, burnt umber, cadmium red, yellow ocher, cadmium orange, cobalt blue, turquoise, and cerulean blue. Oil colors were titanium white, ivory black, raw umber, Payne's gray, cadmium red, burnt umber, yellow ocher, cadmium orange and cobalt blue. Brushes used were Nos. 2 and 3 bristle and a No. 2 sable. The preliminary drawing was done with an F pencil.

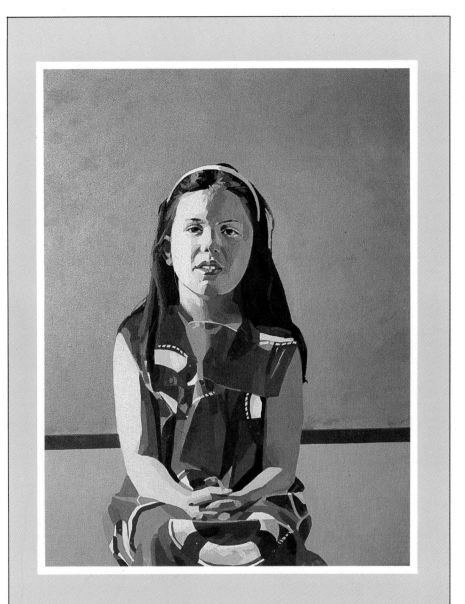

Melissa, from a Photograph

The Wedding Portrait

It is possible to paint creatively from photographs without slavishly reproducing their entire contents or being restricted by the unselective, uniform image usually produced by the camera. For instance, in this wedding photograph the artist has chosen to simplify the background, selecting only certain elements and making these more graphic than they appeared in the original snapshot. The result is a picture with striking formality and an unusual, almost surrealistic setting.

However, the photograph has been given a much more central role in the finished product than is usual for portrait painters. Many painters use photographs as reference only, as the equivalent of rough sketches or shorthand notes, from which to work when the subject is not present. In this case, one particular photograph has been chosen, and its main features have been retained and even built upon, though adapted to give the picture a more personal and permanent feel. The painting represents something consciously put together rather than a recording of a random moment in time.

Because acrylic dries so quickly it is possible to build layer upon layer of thin color rapidly, without long waiting periods between the various stages. This is particularly useful to the portrait painter, who has to depict the subtle and varied tones of skin by building up layers to produce a translucent look.

The artist applied thin color throughout all the early blocking-in stages of this picture, creating a basis to work into in the later stages. First, he established a dark neutral tone for the shadows around the features of the couple and for their hair. This was quickly followed by some approximate dark skin tones and the background. The only splashes of color are the flowers and the bridegroom's tie, and the artist suggested the pinks and greens of the flowers quite early in the process, instead of adding them as a finishing touch. The pink therefore became an integrated tone in this early stage.

The finished picture looks realistic, but is in fact composed of fairly broad areas of tone. The painter cannot see and select detail which has been blurred or lost by the small scale of the photograph. He is faced with the problem of simplifying illegible detail into a flat area of color which, when viewed from a certain distance, becomes an integrated part of the image.

1 A postcard-sized photograph, *right,* was the artist's only reference when painting this souvenir wedding portrait as a present for the bride and groom.

2 The artist starts with an outline pencil drawing on Daler board, and then uses a No. 6 synthetic round brush to block in the darkest areas of the hair and face with a mixture of raw umber and Payne's gray *below left*.

3 Deeper skin tones are blocked in with a mixture of raw umber and burnt sienna. The background is loosely painted in Payne's gray and raw umber with a ³/₄inch synthetic brush *below*.

4 Looking constantly at the photographic reference, the artist develops the skin tones. Because the photographic image is so small, it is not possible to make an exact copy of the image. Instead, the artist translates what is visible in the photograph into general terms rather than making a possibly inaccurate guess at what might be there. Here, *left,* the light flesh tones are blocked in with a mixture of white, raw umber and burnt sienna and cobalt blue.

5 A touch of cadmium red is mixed with white for the flowers. The clothes are applied in broad terms with a large brush *above.* As the color is applied, the artist uses a clean wet brush to alter the tones within the clothing by diluting the lighter areas.

6 The painting is taking shape, with the broad areas of color and tone already established *right.* Because acrylic dries so quickly, this underpainting is ready to be developed, and the artist can start to add detail and make final adjustments immediately.

MASKING LINES

To paint the panes of the gray background window, the artist uses thin strips of masking tape. In order to obtain an even, mechanical line, it is essential that the width of the strip be consistent. The strips of tape are pressed firmly onto the support to stop the color from seeping underneath. The area covered by the tape will be protected and therefore unaffected by any color applied over it. When using masking tape, you should mix the paint to a thick, creamy consistency, since watery color will run under it and spoil the clean edge.

7 *Left,* skin and hair are treated in approximate terms. Because the image is enlarged from a photograph, the planes of light and shade cannot be accurately blended, and the artist makes no attempt to obtain a tidy finish.

8 The artist develops the tonal depth across the whole painting *below left.* Flesh tones are strengthened, and dark gray shadows across the front of the groom lend a feeling of form and solidity to the subject. The groom's tie adds a dash of color.

What the artist used

A palette of cobalt blue, Payne's gray, cadmium red medium, yellow ocher, burnt sienna, black, raw umber, titanium white, and cadmium orange was chosen for this double portrait. The artist worked on Daler board, measuring 22in × 18in, using a ³/₄inch brush for the large expanses of color. Other brushes include sable rounds, Nos. 4 and 6; bristle flats, Nos. 4, 6 and 8; and a No. 6 round synthetic. An F pencil was used for the initial drawing.

The Wedding Portrait

Pippa in a Pink Shirt

The texture of the paint is very much part of this portrait of a girl in a pink shirt. There was comparatively little drawing of detail before the application of the paint, which has been applied in thick strokes with brush and palette knife. The artist used the direction of the paintstrokes to describe the form and contours of the subject. The thick — or impastoed — surface gives a full and lively appearance.

Impasto done with oil paints has always suffered from the problem of being so slow-drying — exceptionally thick paint can take months to dry completely. Acrylic paint, on the other hand, is ideal for this type of painting and has become popular with modern painters who want to create impasto effects. It is best not to try to move or manipulate acrylic paint once it has been applied to the support. Impastoed acrylic has a crisp, fresh appearance which can be destroyed by attempting to move it while it is drying.

The artist began by doing a very quick drawing in charcoal, and then roughing in with a large brush those areas of background immediately surrounding the figure. This was done with broad, textural strokes of color. The artist was then able to establish some initial tones on the figure — flesh, skin and shirt. The paint-strokes were left sketchy and unfinished, to maintain the fresh, spontaneous paint surface. The artist built up the flesh tones with a large brush in broad planes of cool mauves and warm pinks which picked up the color of the shirt. Instead of mixing smooth blended color, he often applied partially mixed, raw paint

scraped from the palette with a knife, incorporating accidental streaks of color to give a freshness to the whole.

By comparison, there is more detail in the facial features, which have been delineated with a small bristle brush. This brings the face into focus and provides a contrast with the sketchy treatment of the clothing and background.

1 To set off the bright pink shirt to advantage, our artist asked the model to sit in neutral-colored surroundings, against a white wall *right*.

2 Working on primed Masonite, the artist starts by sketching in the basic composition with charcoal *below*. Mistakes are corrected by rubbing out the lines and redrawing.

3 Before embarking on the figure, the artist first establishes some of the background tones *above*. All other colors and tones can be related to these initial marks.

4 The cooler skin tones are blocked in with a No. 8 bristle brush *left*. These cool shadow tones are mixed from white, yellow ocher, and crimson — the lighter highlights are predominantly white and yellow ocher with a touch of burnt sienna.

5 A soft sable brush is used to define the contours of the lips and inside edge of the mouth *below*. This artist applies color in short, thick strokes, frequently defining the outline and linear features in a darker color. Patches of white canvas primer are occasionally allowed to show through between the dense paint marks.

PAINTING WITH A KNIFE

Painting knives and palette knives are especially useful for applying thick, impastoed color to create a lively and spontaneous paint surface. Here the artist uses a painting knife to lay in the pink blouse and background area. Acrylics lend themselves to this approach, being quick-drying and therefore ideal for direct, immediate color application which requires no further working on the canvas.

For an especially thick, textural effect, the acrylic paint can be mixed with texture or modeling paste. This is thicker than the actual paint and transforms the color into a stiff substance which retains the shape of the knife.

6 The artist works across the canvas, developing the background in relation to the bright pink of the girl's shirt *left*. The broad folds of fabric are applied with a painting knife, creating solid wedges of flat color which help to create a richly varied surface texture. Painting knives are available in a range of sizes — some types are more flexible than others — and are invaluable when solid or smooth areas of color are required.

What the artist used

The artist worked on the smooth side of masonite, measuring 30in × 24cm and primed with acrylic gesso. The acrylic colors — white, ultramarine, Hooker's green, burnt sienna, yellow ocher, raw sienna, black, crimson, and permanent rose — were applied with flat bristle brushes, Nos. 6, 8 and 10, and a No. 4 sable round.

Pippa in a Pink Shirt

Pause from Work

In this portrait, a complete change from the formal type, the subject pauses for a break from work in her busy environment. The picture makes this immediately clear, in other words, the artist has set out to "tell a story." In doing this, he is following a well-established tradition of portrait painting. The Dutch Master, Jan Vermeer (1632-75), specialized in placing figures in everyday settings which instantly established their jobs and roles in life: some doing housework, some playing musical instruments, and so on. One of the most famous of these genre paintings is *Maid Servant Pouring Milk*.

But, like most paintings, the picture here is not simply a narrative or a portrayal of the woman herself; it is a study in neutral colors. Grays and beiges run quietly and harmoniously through the background, and the fawn of the wall is echoed in the reflections in the glass and video screen. Moreover, the area around the typewriter and glass could be isolated as a tiny still life in its own right — just as in some of the Dutch Masters' works, objects such as food, jugs and kitchen utensils could form miniature still lifes within a bigger picture.

Because this is a picture of an interior as well as a portrait, the setting is important. The background does not exist simply as a backdrop — its detail is a crucial part of the whole. The artist has avoided treating the figure differently from the rest of the composition. The flesh colors of the face and arms are simplified to a very limited range of tones so that the figure does not stand out too much from everything else.

Graphic devices have been used to a considerable extent here. The artist has used flat areas and planes of tone to suggest rounded form, rather than building up a gradual blend — the forearm is divided into three distinct tones of light, medium and dark. In another graphic formula, the artist has used the direction of the red lines on the check shirt to describe the three-dimensional volume of the body underneath. He simply painted an area of pale gray shadow on the space occupied by the shirt, and then relied almost entirely on the red lines.

1 This informal portrait of the young woman pausing from work in her busy environment was painted from the photograph *right*.

2 *Left*, a pre-drawn tracing paper grid, available from graphic suppliers, is used to insure an accurately transferred image. The artist lays the grid on the photograph, then draws a corresponding number of squares on the support. The image is transferred square by square.

3 When the detailed drawing is complete, the artist starts to block in color. Dark hair tones are painted in black, raw umber, burnt sienna, titanium white, and cobalt blue *above*. The artist works accurately with a No. 4 flat bristle brush and a No. 6 synthetic round brush.

4 When the lighter hair tone is established, the artist blocks in the background color *right*. This is done to eliminate the distracting whiteness of the primer. The overwhelming expanse of bright white makes it difficult to assess the real value of new tones and colors as they are applied, and the artist is anxious to establish an accurate middle tone.

5 The light hair tones are elaborated to reflect some of the surrounding background color. With a mixture of Hooker's green, ivory black, and raw umber, the artist carefully paints in the shape of the climbing plant *above*. Traces of the background color are introduced into the leaves.

6 Chrome orange, yellow ocher, cadmium red and cobalt blue make the basic skin tone *right*. Working closely from the photograph, the artist blocks in the shaded side of the face. The success of the portrait depends on absolute accuracy when picking out the shapes of the various planes.

MASKING SHAPES

For foliage and other complicated and repeated shapes, crisply defined edges can be effective. Here the artist has selected a few leaves, giving them a clean, cut-out edge which "lifts" the otherwise flat mass of foliage, creating the illusion that all the leaves are more finished than they actually are.

Wide masking tape is used for this, and the leaf shapes are cut out with a sharp craft knife. The tape is pressed firmly into position and the thickish light green paint applied with a bristle brush. The tape is removed when the paint is dry.

7 A lighter, "middle" skin tone is mixed by adding white to the basic color. This is established in relation to the dark shadow area *left.*

8 The finished face is made up of just three basic tones — light, medium, and dark — carefully rendered to describe the facial form *above.*

9 Gray wash is applied to the shadow areas of the shirt. The color is thin enough to allow the drawn stripes to show through (this drawing acts as a guide to the painted red stripes). Using thin, flowing lines the artist paints in the checked pattern in cadmium red with a No. 3 sable brush *below*. The direction of the stripes is important because it describes the underlying form.

10 The figure and most of the background is now complete *below*. The bright red check becomes a focal point of the painting, drawing the viewer's eye toward the young woman, the subject of the portrait.

11 In muted, neutral colors, the artist starts to block in the objects on the desk *bottom*. The colors reflect the surrounding wall color and some of the neutral tones in the composition.

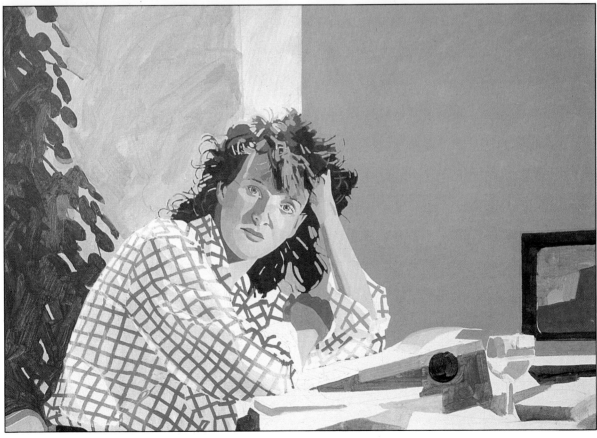

12 The collection of objects on the young woman's desk forms a tonal composition, a miniature still life within the main painting *right*. This arrangement adds an unusual touch without drawing attention from the subject. Notice how the colorless nature of the wine glass is suggested by the use of distorted shapes of various background colors; the rounded shape of the glass is indicated by the use of well-observed shapes of flat tone.

13 Using a plastic ruler, the artist carefully paints five lines on the shade *above*. To paint continuous, even lines in this way, it is necessary to mix the paint to a thin, runny consistency. Here the artist uses a No. 6 synthetic brush, holding the ruler off the surface of the painting. If the loaded brush comes into contact with the edge of the ruler while the ruler is resting on the support, the paint will form blobs and run underneath.

14 A close-up of the woman's face shows how the form is systematically built up from flat patches of color *right*. By making a detailed and accurate drawing of the subject in the early stages, the artist was free to manipulate the limited range of tones in order to create a solid, convincing form. Strong, directional light illuminates one side of the face, emphasizing the contrast between the light and dark tones.

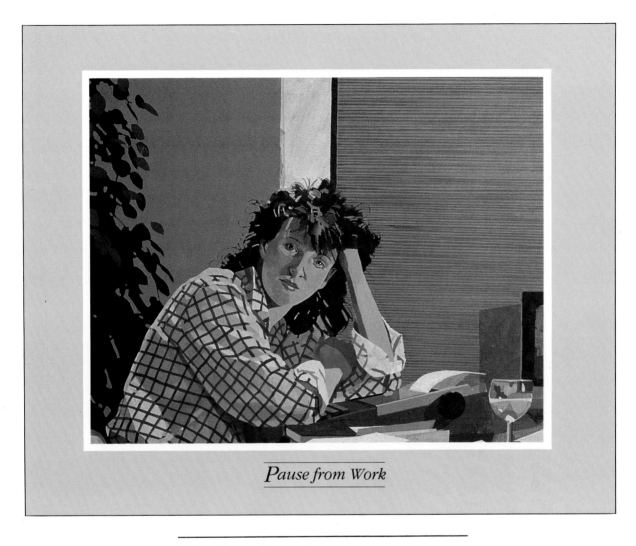

Pause from Work

What the artist used

For this portrait the artist worked on Daler board measuring 25in × 30in. The board was primed for use with either oil or acrylic paints. This was supported on a "Gallery" studio easel for the duration of the painting. An initial pencil drawing was made with a F graphite pencil. The artist worked from a palette of ivory black, raw umber, burnt sienna, titanium white, cobalt blue, Payne's gray, Hooker's green, chrome orange, yellow ocher, cadmium red and cadmium yellow. He used a selection of brushes, the main ones being a No. 4 flat bristle, and a No. 6 synthetic round. Most of the details and linear work, such as the precise leaf shapes, were painted with a No. 2 sable brush.

Family Group

The picture shown here is in fact a preliminary sketch, done in acrylic, which will be used later as the basis for a commissioned painting. Acrylic is ideal for this type of sketch, as its quick-drying quality allows color and tone to be changed readily.

"Note-taking" is how the artist refers to this form of sketching with acrylic. The sketch has been put together from rough pencil drawings and a selection of photographs. The artist has experimented with these elements to see how they work together, in an attempt to arrive at a satisfactory composition. The sketch also provides an opportunity to try out colors and tones.

A sketch of this kind is a useful way of approaching a larger portrait, especially a commissioned one in which it is risky to leave too much to chance. However, the artist will have to overcome the problem of transforming the sketch into a larger painting. He himself has pointed out that "what works on a small scale does not always work on a large one." For instance, the faces of the subjects have been reduced to the barest essentials. The artist will have to return to detailed photographs to develop the features and character of the individuals.

The members of this family particularly wanted to be portrayed in front of their home. The artist has treated the house in such a way that it dominates the background. It is built up with big geometric shapes of starkly contrasting tone. He has offset this with the bright blue reflections of the windowpanes, which pick out the blues appearing in the clothes of three of the subjects.

The grouping plays an important part in this picture. The artist has avoided a "snapshot" type of informality, in order to produce a more considered, permanent-looking product. He has placed the group formally, with one exception — a deliberate means of providing a diversion. The figure on the right, instead of sitting next to the others on the seat, is perched casually on the arm of the bench with the direction of the arms and legs pointing downward toward the corner of the composition. The spiral staircase and the wrought-iron window balconies provide a delicate, linear relief which contrasts with the solid areas of tone making up the rest of the picture.

1 The family, *right,* asked our artist to paint their group portrait. This painting is a preliminary color sketch for the main commission.

2 Combining information from two photographs — one of the family, one of their home — the artist puts together a composition with the members of the family sitting in front of the house. He makes a detailed line drawing directly on the support and starts to block in the dark tones with a thin mixture of ivory black and raw umber *right.*

SIMPLIFYING THE FACE

For quick color sketches, or paintings in which the figure is small and relatively unimportant, it is sometimes useful to try and see, and then paint, the face into the simplest possible terms without losing its identity or form.

If we follow the progress of one of the faces in this group portrait, we see how the artist tackled this problem. The shadow areas are established first in a thin mixture of raw umber and ivory black. Light and medium flesh tones are then added to this, each area of tone being represented by one or two simple brushstrokes.

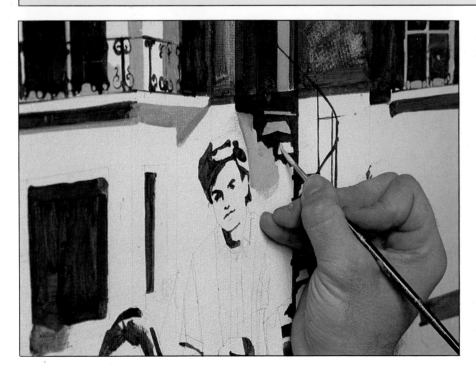

3 Starting with the background, the artist continues to fill in small areas of tone and color *left*. The main house tones are Payne's gray, raw umber, white, and yellow ocher. Window reflections are cerulean blue, Payne's gray and white. A No. 2 brush is used for fine details. Larger areas are painted with a No. 3 flat bristle. Linear details, such as the spiral staircase and wrought-iron balcony, are important to the composition, and painted with care and precision.

4 The artist starts to block in the flesh tones and shadow areas of clothing *right*. Flesh is mixed from white, chrome orange, yellow ocher, cadmium red, and cobalt blue.

5 *Below left,* remaining areas are blocked in, each one carefully related to the rest of the painting. The major areas are now established, and the picture is ready to receive some finishing touches and final details.

6 A No. 2 sable brush is used to refine the tonal planes of the faces. For a preliminary sketch, such as this, the general distribution of tone is more important than exact detail *below right*.

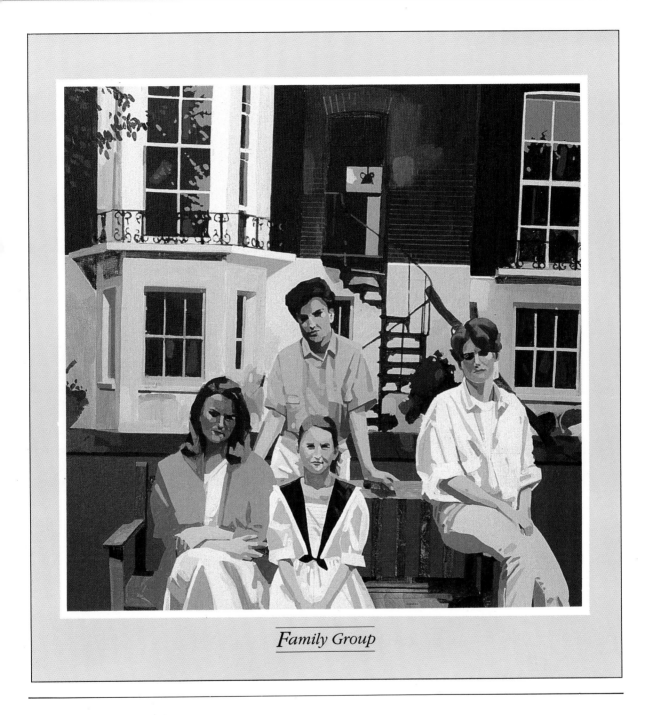

Family Group

What the artist used

A Daler board, cut down to 20in square was the support. Ivory black, raw umber, Payne's gray, titanium white, yellow ocher, cerulean blue, permanent green bright, chrome orange, cadmium red, and cobalt blue were applied with sable brushes Nos. 2, 4 and 6; and flat bristle brushes, Nos. 4, 6, 8.

CHAPTER EIGHT

WATERCOLOR AND GOUACHE

Watercolor is a unique and somewhat unpredictable medium which has always held a special fascination for artists. The element of uncertainty and the accidental effects often achieved with watercolor paints make them exciting to use, and watercolor paintings have a beautiful translucence impossible to achieve in any other medium. Many of the Old Masters used watercolor to make preliminary sketches before embarking on larger oil paintings, but others painted in watercolor alone, using it as a medium in its own right.

There are two types of watercolor, both of which are soluble and bound with gum arabic. Pure watercolor is transparent, and is applied in thin layers of color, usually on white paper. Gouache, or body color, contains chalk, which makes it opaque. Although the purist approach to watercolor forbids the use of white paint or body color, many artists have successfully combined the two.

A comparison between the portrait of the child on page 103 and that of the young man on page 123 provides an example. The former is worked mainly in pure watercolor, the artist building up the image in thin washes of paint and using the light tone of the paper as a basis for the shirt and the highlights on the face and hair. She worked in the traditional watercolor manner, from light to dark, to produce a delicate portrait from transparent layers of color. The second portrait, a young man in a red T-shirt, was painted in gouache, and the difference between the two paintings is immediately apparent. Here the color is opaque, and the artist has used light tones over dark ones to establish the form of the subject, painting pale highlights onto the darker red of the shirt, and using solid blocks of opaque color for the skin tones.

Materials

Watercolors are made from pigments mixed with gum arabic and water. These pigments may be animal, vegetable or mineral, and their quality is always reflected in the price of the paint.

In one respect the watercolorist is lucky, because both the colors and the brushes, once purchased, last a long time. Most artists work with a limited range of paint, and a reasonable range of well-chosen soft brushes is perfectly adequate for most purposes.

Supports

Watercolor paper comes in various sizes, from pocket-sized pads to very large sheets. These differ considerably in thickness and are designated by their weight per ream (500 sheets). Imperial-size sheets, which measure about 22 × 30 in are used for the measuring. The lightest watercolor paper is 72lb; the heaviest is 400lb. The best watercolor paper comes from Europe and is sized metrically, according to the number of grams per square meter (gsm) in a ream.

Lightweight and cheap papers should always be stretched before use. Failure to do this will result in buckled paper and uneven colors as the paper stretches where the wet paint is applied to it. To stretch a paper, first soak it completely, either in a bath of water or under the tap. Lay the wet paper on a drawing board and tape the edges down with gummed paper strip. The paper should be allowed to dry naturally and will normally be ready for use after a few hours. Properly stretched paper will not wrinkle, however wet your colors are. With thicker and better-quality papers, stretching is usually unnecessary.

WATERCOLOR
SKETCHING BLOCK

STRETCHED PAPER

LUMA CONCENTRATED WATERCOLOR

WATERCOLOR
SKETCHBOOKS

The texture of watercolor papers, which varies widely, is important. Some are very rough, with an irregular, "pitted" surface which is favored by many painters. Others are completely smooth, and are generally preferred by graphic artists.

Handmade papers, usually identifiable by their irregular edges, are superior to those manufactured on a machine, and are, of course, much more expensive. They are often made of linen rag and are free from many of the impurities contained in factory-produced paper. To find out which is the right side — the side which has been sized — hold the sheet up to the light and look for the watermark of the maker's name. This should read the right way around.

Machine-made papers are usually cheaper, and the better quality ones are very good indeed. They are available in three main categories — Hot Pressed, Cold Pressed (also called Not), and Rough. The Hot Pressed type tends to be very smooth, and is suitable only where a particularly flat finish is required. The most popular is Cold Pressed, and the majority of watercolor papers fall into this category. Rough paper, as the name suggests, has a very irregular surface and is used when a particularly rugged effect is required.

Watercolor papers are traditionally white or off-white. Coloured or tinted paper is sometimes used for gouache and other opaque paints.

Paints

Genuine watercolor contains no chalk or other opaque ingredient which would threaten its pure, transparent quality. It is sold in four forms: pans or half-pans of moist color, cakes of dry color, tubes, and bottles of liquid color.

WATERCOLOR
PAPERS

HOT-PRESSED

COLD-PRESSED

ROUGH

CONCENTRATED WATERCOLOR

SYNTHETIC ROUND NO.5   SABLE ROUND NO.6

SYNTHETIC ROUND NO.18

FINE PURE SABLE   PURE SABLE BRIGHT

GLASS OF WATER

Dry cakes are the least expensive, but are usually inferior and require much"working" with water before yielding a strong color. Pans or tubes are the professional's choice, and they can be bought either in boxes or individually. Liquid colors, often concentrated, come in small bottles, some of which have a dropper, allowing greater control over the strongly tinted fluid.

Gouache usually comes in tubes and, like watercolor, is available in a wide range of colors. It is an opaque medium, used for its good colors and strong covering powers. Unlike pure watercolor gouache allows you to paint light colors over dark ones. It dries lighter than it appears when wet, with a mat, slightly pastel finish. Powder color and poster paints are occasionally used instead of gouache, but their color and texture bear little resemblance to the real thing.

Unfortunately, there is no substitute for pure watercolor, and only the best quality pigments will produce the superior artists' color. A students' range is available, and is, of course, cheaper, but these paints are noticeably inferior.

Brushes

WATERCOLOR BOX

The best watercolor brushes are made from the sable brushes, the hair of which comes from the tail of the kolinsky, a small mammal living in certain areas of the USSR and China. Because of the inevitably high price of these brushes, manufacturers sell a brush which combines sable with other types of bristle — often the slightly stiffer ox hair, which comes from the ox's ears. Camelhair, squirrel, mongoose and the many good synthetic varieties now on the market are all good alternatives, although none of them possesses the springy quality found in pure sable.

TUBES OF WATERCOLOR

SKETCHING BOX WITH WATER RESERVOIR

GOAT HAIR BLENDER

SHORT BRISTLE
BRUSH FOR STIPPLING

SMALL DECORATOR'S BRUSH

WATERCOLOR
BOX

SYNTHETIC BRIGHT

HALF PANS

WATERCOLOR
MEDIUM

CERAMIC DISH

GUM WATER

MASKING FLUID

GUM ARABIC

Brushes range from the very tiny No. 000, usually used for detailed retouching work, to No. 14 and larger. The large sizes are useful for washes and other wide expanses of color. The numbers are usually printed on the brush handles, although a few ranges are numbered according to a different system.

The most common and the most useful watercolor brushes are the "rounds." Some brushes, known as chisel-ends, have flattened bristles, and these are also useful for applying washes. Japanese and Chinese round, or Sumie, brushes are usually identifiable by their cane or bamboo handles. These are particularly good for the free-flowing, "boneless" style of painting which we associate with oriental watercolors, but can be difficult to manipulate in general use. The fan-shaped brush, with its beautifully regular spread of bristles, is used for special effects and graded washes. A small decorator's brush is useful for applying large areas, and an ordinary toothbrush is an invaluable aid to creating textures and spattering effects.

Palettes and other equipment

Watercolor palettes are generally plastic or ceramic. Those which are incorporated in a paintbox are usually enamel. They have special recesses to hold the different colors and for mixing. Palettes with a thumbhole are especially useful for outdoor work. In the absence of a proper palette, you can use old plates, saucers or any other suitably sized receptacle.

You will also need a drawing board to support the paper (a piece of plywood or blockboard will suffice); other useful items of equipment are a small natural sponge for blotting paint and making textures, plastic water jars with lids for outdoor work, and paper towels for drying brushes and blotting. Gum water and gum arabic are sometimes used to give body and extra sheen to the colors.

Blowing Bubbles

This portrait, in which the artist has transformed a small snapshot into a finished watercolor, relies heavily on the skilled use of certain specific techniques.

The photograph was of the whole figure of the child blowing bubbles, and of the background houses and monkey bars, but the artist used only the upper lefthand corner containing the top part of the child's figure. She overlaid the photograph with a tracing paper grid in order to transfer the image onto a larger scale drawing on another piece of tracing paper. The grid divided the smaller image into 16 squares, and the artist then drew a larger version of each square, thus enlarging the whole scale. Taking the new drawing on tracing paper as a basis, the artist developed and corrected the image, using shading and detail where this was needed to establish the accuracy of the outline.

Now it was time to transfer the drawing to white watercolor board. If she had done this in the usual way, by scribbling over the back of the tracing paper and then going over the outline of the impression with a pencil, she would have ended up with a gray outline and possibly smudges on the paper from the graphite pencil. She avoided this by using iron-oxide paper, which is rather like office carbon paper but produces red-brown outlines. She placed this face down on the support with the tracing paper drawing on top, and then carefully traced the outline with a mechanical lead holder (a special pencil into which a range of leads can be fitted, giving a fine, even line).

The artist began the final painting by laying in a very diluted wash over the background and shadows of the face, hair and clothing. This was almost the same color, with very little variation between the skin tones and the background. She gradually introduced local color when building up with thin washes from light to dark in traditional watercolor manner. For this she used surgical brushes — brushes once used for examining people's eyes. These have the same adaptability as small Chinese paintbrushes.

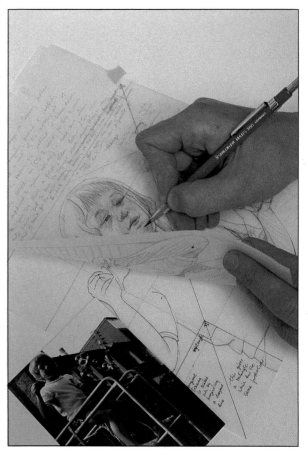

1 A small snapshot, *right,* is the only reference available to the artist for this watercolor portrait of a small child blowing bubbles.

2 Iron-oxide paper is used to enlarge the photographic image to the required size *right*. It is important to start with an absolutely accurate outline, and the artist takes particular care at this stage to obtain a clear, precise image.

3 Working on smooth watercolor board, the artist applies a wash of violet, Indian red, and yellow ocher to the background *top*. This will be strengthened later.

4 The facial shadows are laid in a combination of the background colors *above*. These are slightly darker than the background tone, and will provide depth for subsequent washes.

ENLARGING THE IMAGE

The basis for this watercolor portrait is a color photograph. The artist first constructs a grid on a piece of tracing paper, to cover the relevant area of the photograph. A similar grid, the same size as the proposed painting, is then drawn on a second piece of tracing paper and the image enlarged square by square onto this. Any details to be included in the painting are also included in this enlarged drawing. A sheet of tracing-down paper, sometimes called iron-oxide paper, is placed face down on the support. The enlarged drawing is laid on top of this and the artist carefully follows the lines of the drawing. The tracing-down paper acts like carbon paper, producing a light brownish image which is ready for painting.

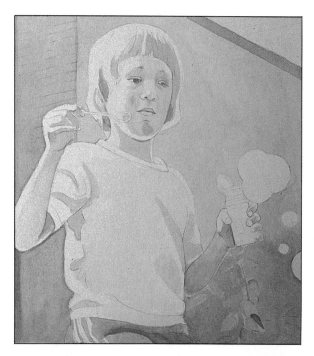

5 This initial wash, *left,* can be applied with a fine sable brush, although our artist actually used a surgical brush, the type once used for examining eyes. This provides the artist with a quality and adaptability similar to that of small Chinese brushes.

What the artist used

The artist used Rowney Artist's watercolors, working mainly with yellow ocher, violet, and Indian red. Other colors were cadmium red, alizarin, ultramarine, Payne's gray and sap green. The support was CS2 watercolor board — the portrait was approximately 8in square. Brushes were sable rounds, Nos. 1, 2, and 4, and a surgical brush. Other materials were iron-oxide paper and a mechanical pencil.

6 *Below left,* shadows are touched in with the point of a No. 2 sable brush, in the traditional watercolor manner of dark over light. The artist moves across the image strengthening the tones — here the shadow between the hair and face is being darkened below.

7 When painting details, the artist frequently finds it difficult to see enough information in the small photograph. The eye is touched in with the point of the No. 2 sable brush, but the artist feels the result is too dark, finding it necessary to strengthen some of the surrounding tones to compensate for this *left.*

8 Most of the painting is built up from the three original colors — violet, yellow ocher and Indian red — although small areas, such as the can of bubbles and the child's jeans, are added in the appropriate local color. To retain the harmony of the composition, the artist develops and strengthens the tones surrounding these brighter colors *above.*

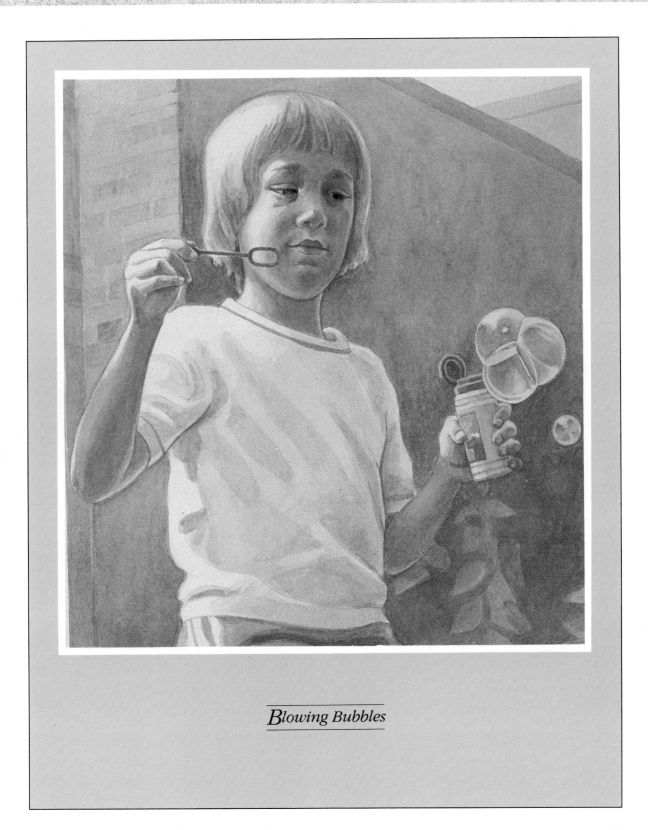

Blowing Bubbles

Against a Striped Blanket

The artist worked from a live model to produce a watercolor in which the colors of the striped blanket in the background play a prominent role. The painting was done deliberately in a low color key, with the image built from loose washes across the paper surface. The brights have therefore been modified into softer pastel tones, yet work in relationship to each other. The charm of the portrait lies in these delicate differences between the overlapping areas of wash.

One of the main considerations in this work was to keep the model in an exact position, because the subtle light and shade tones on the face had to be stable in order for the slight differences to be seen. The model therefore had to be comfortable. She is sitting on a sofa, and the positions of her arms and feet — although not visible in the painting — were chalked so that she could resume the pose after rests. She was also given a fixed point to look at.

The artist worked on a fairly large scale, almost life-size, which involved blocking in large areas on the paper. The character of the picture is very light, with the striped blanket interpreted in subtle tones, and the bright blue shirt reduced to the palest shadows.

The first stage was a line drawing, but a minimal one consisting of the merest outline done with a mechanical lead holder to act as a guide. A very pale graded background wash was applied,

starting with yellow and adding small quantities of cobalt blue as the artist moved from left to right. This gave a sense of dimension to the background, so that it did not remain as a flat color but provided a spatial setting for the subject.

Hair often presents a problem to artists. It is difficult to decide whether to treat it as a mass — as one complete form — or to build it up as separate hairs, giving it an overall texture and trying to work in the many shapes within the main form. Here, the artist treated the tresses as separate forms, blocking in shadow areas and highlights as fairly substantial wedges of color.

1 The artist draped a gaily-colored blanket over the back of the model's chair to brighten this portrait composition *right*.

2 A lightly drawn sketch of the head, shoulders, and background is made on stretched Bockingford watercolor paper *left*. The artist reworks the image, using a kneaded eraser where necessary, in order to get a good likeness of the model at this early stage. When the drawing is complete, the artist rubs out any dark lines, leaving an image that is clear enough to guide the painting, but that will not interfere with the delicate effects of subsequent watercolor washes.

THE EYES

The artist uses a mechancial lead holder to draw the outline of the eyes. This is done carefully, with special attention to the structure of the eye and the underlying eyeball. Working from light to dark, the artist uses a fine brush to paint the narrow shadow thrown by the eyelid across the eyeball.

3 When the drawing is complete, a highly diluted background wash is applied in order to eliminate some of the bright white expanse of paper. The artist begins with pale yellow on one side of the picture, adding small amounts of cobalt blue as she moves across the painting. A No. 2 sable brush is used to block in some of the darker areas of the face with a mixture of Indian red, yellow ocher, and cobalt blue. The hair is mainly yellow ocher, with touches of violet, Indian red, and cobalt *left*.

4 The stripes of the blanket are painted in slightly bolder colors *right*. This provides the artist with a key, a guide to the strength of tones to be used elsewhere in the portrait. The artist uses a No. 2 sable brush throughout the work, painting lines and tiny details with the very tip of the bristles. Most of the color is applied "dry-into-dry", with each layer of wash being allowed to dry before more color is laid on top.

5 Using a mixture of violet, Payne's gray and a touch of Indian red, the artist picks out the darkest shadows of the hair *below*. These are a similar color to the cool shaded area of the face and blouse.

6 The main areas of color and tone are now complete *above*. The artist feels the image is rather weak, lacking solidity and tonal interest. To complete the painting, she strengthens the flesh tones and darkens the clothing. The hair is worked into with a wider range of cool and warm colors, defining the curls and bringing out the texture of the hair.

Against a Striped Blanket

What the artist used

The artist worked on stretched Bockingford watercolor paper measuring 18in × 16in. From a box of watercolor paints, she used Indian red, yellow ocher, violet, Payne's gray, cobalt blue, alizarin, cadmium red, ultramarine, and sap green. She used a mechanical lead holder , a No. 2 sable brush and a kneaded eraser.

Sitting Cross-legged

"Wet-into-dry" is the term used for the technique employed in this portrayal of a young person sitting cross-legged on a kitchen chair. This describes the process of applying a color wash over a dry color, as opposed to "wet-into-wet", in which the colors are allowed to bleed into each other. Because the artist was painting with a lot of wet color, he used a hair drier in between stages to speed up the process.

The artist began with a pencil drawing which indicated the outlines and tonal areas of the subject. He worked into the drawing with the pale flesh tones of the face and hands, using pale washes in a base color of orange, alizarin, burnt umber and yellow ocher. When these were dry the darker tones of the T-shirt were added, followed by the middle tones of the hair in a darker version of the flesh color. As the shadows built up in an increasing variety of tones, the image began to emerge as a solid, recognizable form.

In a slightly unusual approach, the artist filled in the background after the subject was complete. He used the dark color of the background to define and develop the contours of the figure. For instance, a small sable brush was used to pick out the spiky form of the hair and bangs, leaving narrow slivers of white paper as the highlights on the hair. In this way, the darkness of the background was actually used to provide a definitive outline for the central image.

The lettering on the shirt is important in this portrait because it describes the folds and creases and helps to give an impression of the form beneath. Here the artist worked directly by eye, in paint, using his experience to obtain an accurate rendering. Generally it would be necessary to draw the letters in pencil first before committing them to paint.

1 The strong directional light on the seated child, *right,* provides the artist with ample opportunity to use the classical watercolor technique of allowing the white paper to represent highlights.

2 The artist makes a light pencil drawing and starts to apply pale washes of color *right.* Flesh tones are mixed with cadmium orange, alizarin crimson, burnt umber, and yellow ocher; shadows on the clothing are blocked in with cobalt blue, Payne's gray, and ivory black.

3 *Opposite,* a darker flesh color is used for the middle tones of the hair. Shadows are added in raw umber and Payne's gray. Here the artist touches in the lettering on the T-shirt in pure black mixed with gum water.

4 *Far right,* the artist works across the image, strengthening the tones to develop the form. A mixture of black and Payne's gray is used to darken the clothing tones on the shaded side of the subject.

USING THE BACKGROUND TO DEFINE SHAPES

The "negative space" of the background often provides the artist with a good opportunity to redraw and redefine the shape of the subject. Here the artist uses a small brush to take the background color up to the edge of the subject, at the same time tightening up and improving the contours of the boy's face and the line of the leg. Although this method is useful for making small alterations, it is a mistake to attempt any significant changes at this stage.

5 When the basic tones have been established, the background is blocked in with Payne's gray mixed with a little black *below*. Using a No. 2 sable brush to take the paint up to the subject, the artist takes this opportunity to redefine and sharpen the outline of the figure.

6 *Right,* the imposition of the strong, dark background causes some of the figure tones to look weak and faded in comparison. To remedy this, the artist strengthens some of the darkest shadows. For example, the eye and nostril have been picked out with a dense mixture of ivory black and burnt sienna *right.*

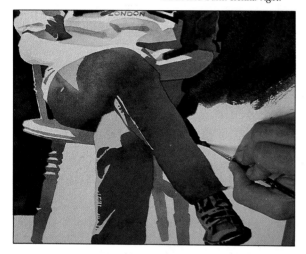

7 Lettering on the T-shirt is painted accurately, the shape of the words being dictated by the folds and creases in the fabric *right.* Gum water is mixed with black paint to create a rich, dense tone — it also causes the paint to dry with a slight sheen. Both gum water and the thicker gum arabic can be used to enliven the normally mat finish of watercolor.

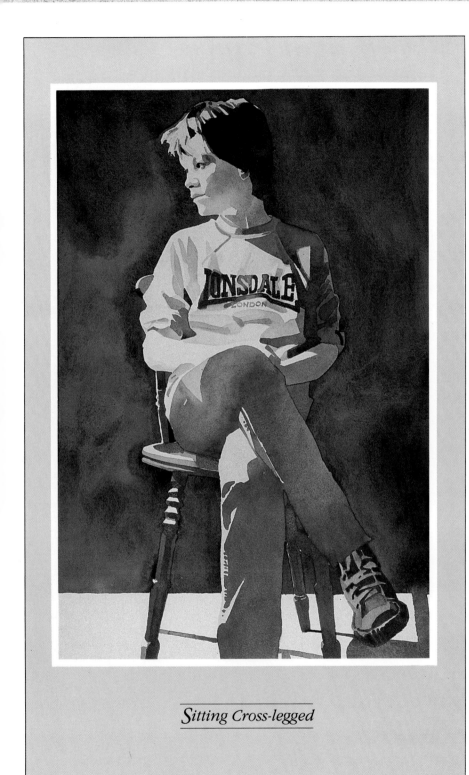

Sitting Cross-legged

What the artist used

A sheet of stretched Bockingford watercolor paper was the support for this young boy's portrait. Standard sizes were unsuitable because the artist needed to work on a slightly narrower rectangle to accommodate the seated figure. He therefore cut the paper to meet his own requirements, making it approximately $25\frac{1}{2}$in$\times 17\frac{1}{2}$in. Most of the portrait was painted with a No. 2 round sable brush, although the artist used smaller sizes, Nos. 0 and 1, for the lettering and some of the finer areas of color. Colors were ivory black, Payne's gray, cadmium orange, alizarin crimson, burnt umber, yellow ocher, raw umber, burnt sienna, and cobalt blue. The lettering on the T-shirt and some of the deep clothing shadows were strengthened with the addition addition of gum water. A preliminary drawing was made with an F pencil, and the artist used a hairdrier to speed up the drying process between stages.

Portrait of Paul

A quill pen, made from a goose feather, was used to make the initial drawing of this portrait. Quills are often used when a natural, undulating line is required, since by turning the quill it is possible to vary the width of the line, achieving a swelling and diminishing effect. Paint, watered down to a very thin consistency, was used with the quill in this case.

The quill drawing was done quickly, exploring spontaneous effects without much thought for form, and looking deeply into the face in a linear way, seeking the most interesting contours. Using a Chinese brush, the artist then applied thin washes of color across the image, supplementing the quill by softening the drawing in places with a little clean water.

This artist likes to work close to the subject, since this enables her to observe contours and lines within the main outline. She is less interested in light and shade and the tonal representation of form. Character portrayed through line is one of her objectives, and if a line is wrong she can draw over it repeatedly until a contour emerges, increasing the strength of the line so that the darker ones dominate. It is almost the opposite of the technique used by some other painters illustrated in this book; for instance, the previous painting, on page 111, begins with a precise single outline which is systematically worked into with areas of color.

The artist here has suggested form in several places by using the lines drawn by the quill. She has used short, broad strokes to describe the shape and texture of the subject's hair, thus avoiding a formal or analytic approach, yet giving depth and a sense of volume to an almost wholly linear image.

1 This artist is concerned with the contours within the subject's face and prefers the simple front view, *right,* to a more elaborate pose.

3 Color is drawn directly on the paper without any preliminary pencil drawing. The loose lines of the quill pen describe the internal contours of the face *below.*

2 *Above,* the artist works from three diluted watercolor mixtures: raw sienna and cobalt blue; Prussian blue and cadmium red; cadmium yellow and yellow ocher.

4 Mistakes are difficult to remove, but wrong lines can be softened with water. Here, *right,* the artist uses a Rowney No. 9 (series 40) brush to lighten an incorrect line before redrawing.

5 Selected areas of local color are applied with a Chinese brush. The color is not literal but is a spontaneous reaction to what the artist sees. *Below,* she applies a warm orange to the neck.

6 The background is worked with a Chinese brush and a No. 9 sable round *right.* No attempt is made to create flat, even color. Instead, the artist exploits the textural brushmarks.

DRAWING WITH A QUILL

A purchased quill was used for the initial outlines of this watercolor sketch. Quills are usually made from goose or swan feathers — you can make your own by cutting a diagonal tip with a sharp blade or scalpel. They are particularly effective for drawing on rough or heavily textured paper and, unlike a pen, do not catch on the fibers but glide smoothly across the surface to produce an irregular but flowing line.

Here the artist is using the quill for the fine, sketchy outline and for adding broader areas of dark texture to the hair.

7 Light and tone are not important aspects of this portrait. The painting so far reflects the artist's prime interest in the linear qualities of the face *left*.

8 A Chinese brush is used to apply color to the jacket *above*. Again, the emphasis is on the linear and directional rather than on a literal representation of the local color.

What the artist used

For this watercolor portrait, the artist chose to work on Langton watercolor paper, measuring approximately 12in×10in. On this occasion she worked with a purchased quill pen, although she often makes her own from a goose's or swan's feather, cutting this diagonally near the tip with a sharp blade. Brushes used were a Rowney No. 9 sable (series 40) and a Chinese brush. Colors were watercolor tubes — raw sienna, cobalt blue, Prussian blue, cadmium red, cadmium yellow and yellow ocher. These were mixed in separate ceramic dishes.

Portrait of Paul

Girl with a Pony-tail

The girl is painted in straight profile, with a background of plain white, but the artist has taken two steps to improve the background. She has cropped the composition very closely so that the top of the head and the back of the girl's hair touch the sides, breaking the background into four definite shapes. She has also included a dark, textural background, introducing a pattern of black, white and gray in the bottom section of the composition.

The painting is a small one, enabling the artist to see the image as a whole at a glance and to work tightly, producing controlled shapes and lines.

Although the artist has worked in a traditional watercolor manner, building up tone and color from light to dark, she has broken the rules in one respect. Occasionally she introduced opaque white to represent tiny highlights and to correct mistakes. For this she used a special "bleed-proof" white, which stops the colors beneath from showing through and running into it, as they will with gouache or poster-color white. For instance, the fine white highlight along the girl's collar has been added later with a fine brush because the artist neglected to leave a margin of white paper showing through the color. This type of white is extremely useful when correcting mistakes, but it should be used only in small quantities and only when absolutely necessary, as it tends to destroy the transparent quality of the medium.

An initial fine-line drawing was done for this portrait, using a sharp mechanical lead holder. Because the portrait is a small one, the drawing had to be quite precise, containing enough detail to allow the artist to concentrate on the ensuing build-up of tone and color.

1 The model was sitting against a plain white wall, *right,* although the artist subsequently decided to create a more substantial background.

2 A mechanical lead holder is used to make an initial drawing *right.* This pencil has a fairly hard adjustable lead, making a light, precise line which is particularly suitable for watercolor work. The support is pure white watercolor board (CS2) measuring just 6in×6in, which does not yellow with age. At this stage the artist decides that the composition needs some added background and suggests this with light lines.

3 The profile head fills the rectangular picture area. This forms a series of abstract shapes around the subject, creating a tightly arranged composition with a deliberate lack of empty space around the head. By taking the subject out of the picture area on three sides, the artist makes the remaining "negative" shapes almost as important to the final composition as the face itself. The artist starts to apply color in this wash *left*. Hair tones are mixed from violet, yellow ocher and Payne's gray; the blouse is rose madder, cadmium red, and a touch of Payne's gray.

4 Using a No. 2 sable brush the artist washes in the flesh color in yellow ocher, Payne's gray and rose madder. The shadow tones are painted in precise areas, emphasizing the light highlights of the face and describing the form and underlying structure. The background tones are developed to create a sense of space in the painting *left*. Notice how the color is applied gradually, the initial light washes being built up layer by layer until the correct tone is established.

DARK OVER LIGHT

Because watercolor is transparent, it is difficult or impossible to paint a light color over a darker one successfully. Here a very dilute wash, representing the light areas of hair and the highlights, has been laid over the entire hair area and allowed to dry — in the picture the artist is using the traditional "dark over light" watercolor technique to add shadow areas to the hair.

5 Opaque white is used for tiny highlights. *Above,* the artist uses "bleed-proof" paint for the narrow edge of light on the collar.

6 Face and flesh tones are worked from light to dark, and linear details, such as the eyes, are drawn in with a No. 2 sable brush *right.*

What the artist used

The artist used a sheet of CS2 smooth white watercolor board which is made especially for line and watercolor work. The board retains its color and does not yellow with age. Watercolors were rose madder, cadmium red, violet, Payne's gray, yellow ocher, raw umber, and burnt sienna. Opaque "bleed-proof" white paint was used for some of the smaller highlights (these were kept to a minimum to preserve the transparent quality of the overall image). The artist worked with a No. 2 round sable brush, using the tip of this for linear details and especially tiny areas. A preliminary line drawing was done with a mechanical lead holder.

Girl with a Pony-tail

In a Red T-shirt

This portrait is painted in gouache, an opaque form of watercolor, which enables the artist to paint light colors over darker ones in a way that cannot be done with pure watercolor. The gouache gives a more solid effect, and a slightly chalky finish, particularly on the face tones, which have been blocked in with patches of thick opaque color instead of the watercolor technique of a series of overlaid washes.

Gouache needs care. It is always water-soluble, even when dry, so when painting one color on top of another there is always a risk of disturbing and mixing with the preceding color. For this reason the medium is better suited to quick color sketches than to finished paintings. Notice here how the artist has not attempted to blend in, or tidy up, the planes of color, but has left them as a patchwork of broad, gesturing strokes which work optically as an overall image.

In this portrait the face contains more detail than the rest of the picture, making it the focal point. The background has been left deliberately unfinished, suggesting a hazy though real interior. The artist worked from natural light coming from a window to the right of the model, which helped describe the volume of the figure and the forms within the face.

The artist began by making a drawing with a brush, instead of a preliminary pencil sketch, and the painting grew from this drawing rather than being treated as a separate stage. Thin washes of color were used in conjunction with bold, brushed outlines, causing the image to emerge gradually. The artist used a bristle brush for most of the work, removing the temptation to become lost in particular details to the detriment of the overall composition.

The model was posed in a relaxed position, elbows resting on the arms of a chair, and the artist placed the head slightly to the left of the composition to balance the elements in the picture. Throughout, the work was kept as fluid and free as possible, allowing the artist to make constant adjustments with the opaque color.

1 The model is turned slightly, presenting a three-quarters view to the artist *right*.

2 Instead of starting with a preliminary pencil drawing, the artist begins by drawing directly on the canvas with brush and paint *right*.

3 The artist blocks in basic tones and colors, keeping the image fluid, and constantly changing and readjusting the main elements in this early stage. Here the pants are established as a solid, dark shape with a No. 6 flat bristle brush *right*.

4 This direct approach gives the artist freedom to develop the face as a series of tones. These tonal planes can be changed and moved around on the paper until the form and likeness of the face emerge from the arrangement of lights and darks. Here, *below,* the artist works out the structure and position of the eye.

5 The paint is kept as fluid as possible. As the painting grows out of the initial "drawing", the artist continually returns to the drawing, strengthening the outlines to insure that the structure and form of the figure are not weakened or lost as the tone and color are developed. Because gouache is opaque, it is possible to paint a light tone over a darker one. The artist takes advantage of this quality by working the red tones of the shirt from dark to light. He first establishes the local color in cadmium red, yellow and raw umber, then adds white to this basic mixture in order to paint the highlights *below.* Too much water reduces the covering power of gouache, and the artist takes care to keep the paint at a thick, creamy consistency for maximum opacity.

LIGHT OVER DARK

Gouache contains a lot of chalk, or body color. This makes it opaque, unlike pure watercolor which is transparent. With gouache it is possible to paint extremely light colors, or even white, over a dark base, provided the paint is not diluted too much. In this portrait the artist takes advantage of the opacity to add highlights to the face and arms, and to lay in the light areas of the shirt and pants.

What the artist used

This gouache portrait was painted on a sheet of stretched Bockingford watercolor paper measuring approximately 24in×20in. The artist chose a palette of cadmium red, cadmium orange, alizarin crimson, white, burnt sienna, cadmium yellow, yellow ocher, raw umber, ivory black and Payne's gray. Color was applied with flat bristle brushes, Nos. 2, 4 and 6. The artist used a white dinner plate as a palette.

6 Dried gouache remains soluble. Wet paint may disturb the color underneath, although in this painting, *above*, the loose style makes this unimportant.

7 The composition is considered for its abstract qualities as well as for its more obvious representational function *above*.

In a Red T-shirt

CHAPTER NINE

PASTEL

Pastels are perfect for rapid, on-the-spot sketching, since they have a spontaneity that makes them difficult to rival for a quick color rendering. There are basically two types — the traditional soft pastels which crumble and smudge easily and must be sprayed with fixative, and the more recent oil pastels which are more stable but can be difficult to blend.

Pastel work is sometimes referred to as "drawing," sometimes as "painting." In fact, it falls somewhere between the two. The softest pastels produce an effect which is very similar to that of painting, with the entire surface being covered with solid pigment. Slightly grittier "soft" pastels are also available, and the effect of these is more like that of drawing.

Although pastels have been popular since they first came into general use more than two hundred years ago, they were particularly important to the Impressionists, who saw the possibilities of the brilliant, broken color areas that could be created with them. The works of Edgar Degas (1834-1917) gave the relatively unexploited medium a new importance. He used pastels in bold superimposed layers, developing an ideal combination of line and color. He also devised a technique of steaming the pastel surface to dissolve the pigment into films of color which he then worked with a stiff brush or with his fingers.

INGRES PAPER

PUTTY ERASER

Materials

Pastels are a medium that lies half way between painting and drawing. The traditional pastels are soft and chalky, requiring care both during the execution of the work and afterward, when it is all too easy to smudge the colors. They have qualities in common with chalk and conté crayon, which are sometimes included in the same general category.

Supports

The most important consideration when choosing paper for pastels is the texture. This must be rough enough to provide a "key" or "tooth" for the fine pastel dust to adhere to; otherwise the color literally drops off the paper. Your support should also be a good-quality one; otherwise it will tear and buckle as you work.

Papers that are specially made for pastels have a velvety or sandpaper-like surface. This is ideal, allowing a substantial amount of color to be built up within a single image. Good quality drawing or watercolor paper is perfectly adequate, provided it is coarse enough to take the pastel. Very smooth surfaces are almost always unsuitable, since the pastel slips around the surface and very little actual color will adhere to it.

Tinted papers are excellent for use with pastels. Warm, cool, bright or subtle shades can be exploited to advantage. The tinted paper is allowed to show through between the pastel marks, integrating the composition and contributing to the work in a positive and effective way. Some artists prefer to tint their own paper for pastel work. This can be done by dipping a dampened rag in the crushed ends of pastel sticks and rubbing the paper to produce a toned background for the drawing.

Prepared canvas or "scrim," a thin muslin-type cloth glued to a board or piece of cardboard, is often used for pastel work.

Soft pastels

Soft pastels are powdered pigments mixed with enough gum arabic or resin to bind them together. The word pastel, now widely accepted as meaning anything which is pale or mixed with white, comes from the "paste" of pigment and gum which is molded into the solid sticks and sold either individually or as boxed sets. These sets range from 12 sticks to enormous boxes containing over 300 shades and colors. You can also buy "specialist" sets which are carefully selected to suit particular subjects — one set is sold especially for portrait work.

A reasonable choice of colors is essential, since pastels can only be blended to a degree. Overblending results in loss of brilliance and a clogged paper surface, both of which deaden the natural freshness and spontaneity associated with the medium.

An organized, systematic approach is essential when using pastels. Each color comes in a selection of tones, from very light to dark, and if you cannot immediately lay your hands on the one you want, you will end up using the wrong tone or color and the picture will suffer as a result. If your box does not have compartments for each stick, use a sheet of corrugated cardboard, laying out the pastels according to tone and color so that you can see immediately what is available.

Many artists prefer to make their own pastels from pigment and chalk, since this enables them to choose tones and colors exactly. By mixing a slightly different amount of chalk with each pigment, an enormous range can be made.

SABLE BRUSH NO.11

AEROSOL FIXATIVE

127

TORCHONS

Oil pastels

In this type of pastel the pigment and chalk are mixed with oil instead of gum arabic. Oil pastels are more stable than the traditional soft pastels, being harder and less easy to smudge. Artists who have been used to soft pastels sometimes find oil pastels difficult to use initially because, although the two media are both termed "pastels," they are actually very different to use and produce different results. Oil pastels are particularly good for sketching, where a strong, colorful image is required, and they can also be used in conjunction with oil paints, either for the initial drawing or for rendering final details.

Oil pastels are not easy to blend by using one color over another, since they tend to clog in an uneven mass, but they can sometimes be merged by rubbing. They are soluble in turpentine, and this can be applied directly to the support with a rag or brush to produce a smoothly blended effect.

Care of pastels

Too much pressure causes soft pastels to break, and you can soon end up with a mass of small pieces, most of which are not large enough to hold or manipulate properly. This situation is much easier to salvage if your set is kept systematically in the box, since larger broken pieces can then be put back in their original place without getting lost. Corrugated cardboard is useful for keeping individual sticks separate. Without this, the pastels rub together and it becomes impossible to tell them apart.

Fixative

Soft pastels must be fixed or the picture will become smudged and quickly ruined. The soft, powdery nature of the medium

OIL PASTELS

TURPENTINE

makes it particularly vulnerable, and even pastel drawings framed under glass will disintegrate to some degree without prior fixing. The fixative is sprayed onto the finished work and binds the loose particles of pigment to the ground.

Various adhesive materials have been used as a fixative – in emergencies some artists have used hair spray. The choice depends on the nature of the ground and which medium is being used. Fixative can be bought ready-made in convenient aerosol cans, or it can be bought in bottles, in which case you will need a mouth spray, or atomizer, to apply it.

Fix the work by holding the spray about 12 in away from the drawing, which must be held vertically. Apply the fixative lightly from side to side across the entire surface. Several light coats are better than one heavy one, for a soaking may cause colors to run and affect the crispness of the image. Pastels can be fixed from the back as well as the front, depending on the drawing and the amount of pigment on the surface. You can also use fixative lightly after each stage, although too much will cause the surface to become shiny and unreceptive to further pigment.

Other equipment

A chamois stick and a tortillon (a pencil-shaped stump usually made from tightly rolled paper) are useful for blending and rubbing out fine areas of color. Pastel holders, available from artists' suppliers, can be helpful for holding short sticks and for keeping your hands clean. For sharpening pastel sticks, use sandpaper and for erasing lightly-worked areas, use a kneaded eraser.

Jane

Pastels can be used either in a linear way as a drawing medium or in a more "painterly" way to obtain areas of solid color. The artist here has combined both these approaches, using line to establish the pose and to draw the main characteristics, and then developing selected areas in blocks.

Dark, rich brown paper was chosen for this portrait. This enabled the artist to lay in light skin tones and the highlights of the hair with maximum effect, allowing the tinted paper to show through and suggest shadows and recesses. Choice of paper is particularly important with pastels – darker and tinted papers are often used, since they provide a ready-made middle tone against which the other colors can be set. When using white papers remember that whatever color goes on them will show up darker than the paper background, and the flat plane of white paper has to be counteracted with the pastel. Areas of white showing between pastel strokes tend to "fight with" a solid form; the viewer will always be subconsciously reminded of the white paper and thus be distracted from taking in the complete image.

Jane sits in an armchair, in pensive pose, looking directly out of the picture. The strongest light comes from behind her left shoulder, emphasizing the shape of the back of the neck and the jawline. The background was complex, almost cluttered, but the artist has chosen to ignore this completely, concentrating only on the powerful expression and mood of the pose.

Because pastel comes in chunky sticks, it is often assumed that the medium is best suited to broad strokes and general impressions, but in fact it is possible to render quite delicate and precise details with it, especially when the sticks are sharpened. The hand presented a particular problem in this portrait, because it is a central part of the whole pose and could easily have looked unnatural and awkward. The artist has treated the hand in the context of the face, giving both the same defined planes and highlights, so that the hand guides the viewer's eye around into the enclosed, vignetted composition.

1 The model sits in an informal, though upright, position *right*. She is almost in profile, but a small part of the other side of her face is visible.

2 When working on a medium-toned paper like the one used in this portrait, it is possible to relate all marks to this already established "middle" tone. The artist is therefore able to use white to establish the position of face and hands *right*. This light tone will eventually be integrated into the light flesh tones.

3 Regular diagonal shading from left to right emphasizes the form of the head *above*. At this stage the shading is applied lightly, the artist working across the whole image, marking in key areas of light and shade.

4 For finer areas, such as the shadows under the eyes and around the mouth, the artist changes to colored pencil *top right*. Instead of using neutral tones, the artist chooses cool blues and greens to contrast with the warmly tinted paper.

5 As the drawing nears completion, greater emphasis is put on the face and hand *right*. The flesh tones become more substantial and the artist introduces a range of strong orange-pinks and blue-greens to depict the warm highlights and cool shaded areas of the face.

SOLID TONE WITH PASTEL

The solid areas of tone and color in this picture are built up with short, closely-packed pastel strokes. This is especially necessary when using such darkly tinted paper, because it prevents the paper color from showing through the lighter tones and breaking up and weakening the image. The artist uses the pastels in even, diagonally parallel strokes, allowing greater control over the density of both the tone and the color.

6 *Top,* the artist begins to block in the shoulders and upper part of the jacket. Local color and highlights are filled in with blue; the tinted paper shows through to indicate shadow areas.

7 The flexibility of pastel allows it to be used to depict both line and tone. This close-up, *above,* shows how the artist combines the two techniques.

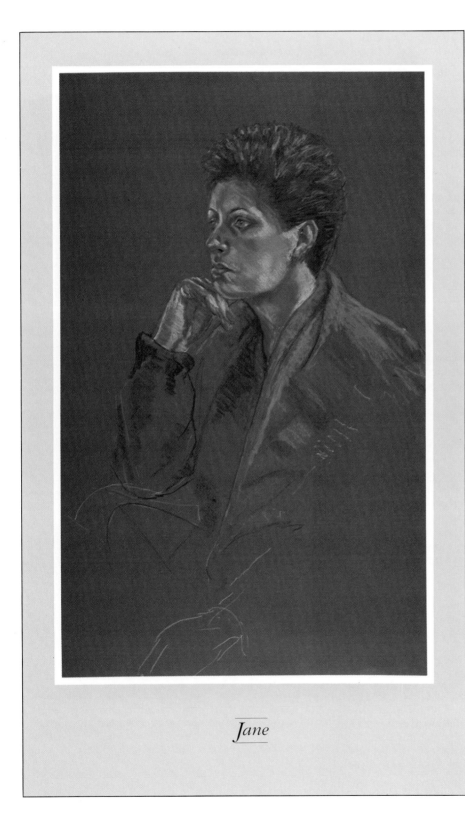

Jane

What the artist used

Toned paper measuring 14in×20in was used for this pastel portrait. The artist chose the warm, deep brown because it provided maximum contrast with the cold blue of the model's jacket. The dark tint also allowed the artist to apply the flesh tones as solid areas of light color. Tinted papers are ideal for use with pastels. They provide an instant "middle" tone, allowing the artist to begin work with a complete tonal range, including white and black. Most pastel artists avoid working on white or off-white paper because it is usually necessary to break down the paper surface into workable tones before the image can be established. With pastels, this is a messy job, often making it difficult to keep subsequent colors clear and bright. Soft pastels were from a boxed set of 72 assorted colors manufactured by Rowney. Blue, green, gray and purple colored pencils were used for smaller areas of flesh shadows.

John 1 and 2

Pastels do not restrict the artist's scale, as these very large portraits illustrate. If you look at the size of the artist's hand compared with the emerging facial features, you will see how the pastels can be used on a grand scale, producing in this case a dramatic effect.

Both these portraits were done on large sheets of primed cardboard. The first was given a thin coat of white oil paint and the second was primed with dark oil paint. In both cases, instead of beginning with an outline that would establish the rough areas of the composition, the artist started from the inside of the features and worked outward. She blocked in the areas of the nose and central face, using the side of the pastel to obtain a broad area of broken color to work into.

The final effect was made even more dramatic by the fact that the subject's face fills the entire picture area, especially in the first picture. Because the area is so large, the artist is unable to see the whole image while she is working, so she moves across the entire picture, placing marks to denote the related positions of the features and contours within the face. The marks were strokes of bold color — each one denoting just a portion of a particular feature — which were related together as the picture developed.

In both pictures the color is intuitive. The artist has greatly exaggerated the reflected tones and colors visible on the actual subject, interpreting these in bright and vibrant terms. She has built up hue upon hue as the lines have become more intense and closely packed, so that in places the lines gradually merge into solid areas of tone.

In the first portrait the various bright colors of the built-up lines mix optically to produce a shimmering and delicate interpretation of the skin tones. Orange and yellow, for instance, are overlaid to create a vibrant orange. Because of the way the drawing has been built up, the artist has avoided the clogged, overworked paper surface which all too often is the result of enthusiastic but inexperienced work with pastels.

The use of color in the second portrait is equally personal and idiosyncratic, but here the dark-toned background has enabled the artist to use a lot of white with the bright pastel colors. The result is a luminous, slightly unearthly portrait.

1 A close-up view of John's face, *right*, provided the artist with enough visual inspiration to produce two large and colorful pastel portraits.

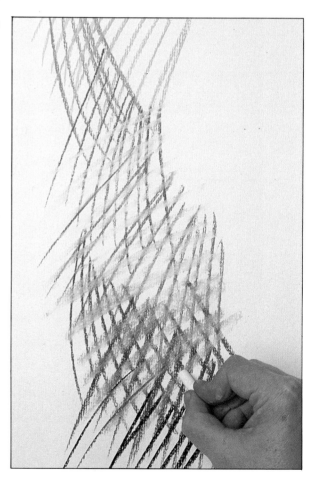

2 Working directly on the large sheet of cardboard treated with white oil primer, the artist starts by boldly cross-hatching areas of bright color *right*. There is no preliminary drawing.

OPTICAL COLOR BLENDING

Pastel colors can be blended by rubbing them together, usually with cloth, tissue or the fingers. Or — as the artist has done in this portrait — they can be blended optically, to mix in the eye of the viewer rather than being actually blended together on the support. Here the artist has relied heavily on drawing, on the linear marks made by the pastels, to build up the structure of the subject's face. She mixes colors by laying thin meshes of pure pastel, one on top of the other, to create new and brilliant hues. For example, the rich greens in the beard and mustache are the result of dense layers of blue and yellow lines; many of the mauve and purple tones come from blue and pink; and the vivid oranges of the lips and skin tones are "mixed" from primary red and yellow.

3 Color is intuitive. The artist is not interested in representing the actual flesh tones, but works from a personal selection of vivid colors *above*.

4 The image emerges from the mass of sketchy lines *right,* and the artist frequently stands back from the work in order to get an overall view of the large-scale portrait.

5 Colors are often mixed "optically." For instance, yellow is worked over red to create a bright orange *above left*. This method produces exceptionally vibrant and luminous colors.

6 *Above,* working on such a large scale helps the artist to maintain a loose, spontaneous approach. The artist continues to build up the image, creating form by intensifying the cross-hatched areas of color.

7 White chalk emphasizes the eye *left.* The chalk is brighter than the dullish white of the primed Masonite, and stands out strikingly from the surrounding colors.

What the artist used

The artist worked from a boxed set of 24 soft pastels, working mainly in bright reds, orange, green, violet, blue, and yellow. White chalk was used for the eyes and occasional highlight. The artist worked on a sheet of primed cardboard measuring 36in×24in. Primed cardboard is an unusual support for pastel work, but in this case the artist was more interested in creating a lively, textural interpretation of the subject than an exact representation of the subject, and therefore chose this slightly coarse surface. The work was supported on a Rowney's Norwich easel, which enabled the artist to stand back frequently from her work.

John 1

BLENDING LARGE AREAS OF COLOR

In this large pastel portrait the artist has used her hand and fingers to blend colors in the face, background and clothing. Care was taken not to overdo these smooth areas, since too much blending can make the image blurred and soggy, tending to destroy the structure of the drawing. In this case enough of the coarse pastel strokes are left showing through to preserve the form and structure of the subject, as well as providing textural contrast. The drawing was sprayed lightly with fixative between stages to prevent the bright color and pure white from smudging as the artist worked. It was then re-fixed on completion to protect it.

1 The artist embarks on a second pastel portrait, working on the same large scale as before *top*. For this painting she chooses a dark support — pieces of cardboard treated with a coat of deep blue oil primer.

2 Using broad strokes of pastel, the artist begins by establishing the main facial tones *above*. There is a predominance of white and pastel tones here, contrasting with the dark blue of the support.

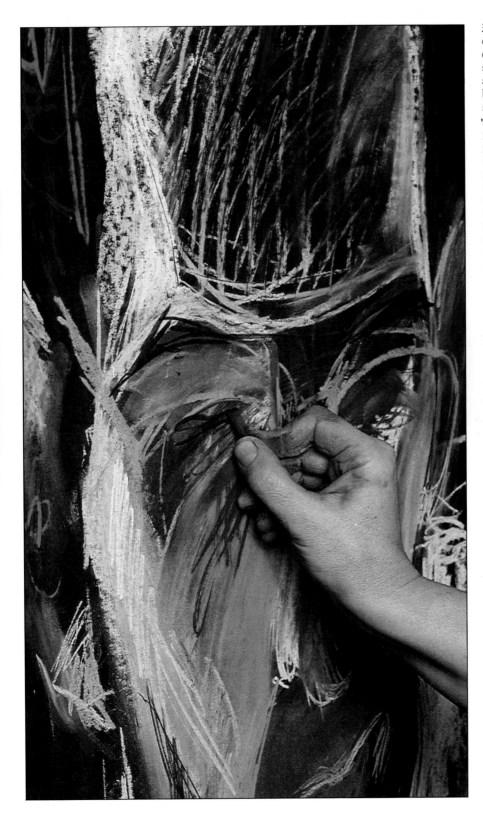

3 Using black chalk, the artist draws in the facial features. This drawn linear detail, superimposed on the blended areas of light tone and color, brings the entire image into sharp focus *left*. The technique illustrates the flexibility of pastels, which can be used to produce either linear effects (as the artist demonstrates in the preceding pastel portrait) or to establish extensive blocks of solid color and tone. Although it is generally assumed that pastel is best suited to fairly broad treatment, considerable linear detail can be obtained by sharpening the pastels or by using the sharp edge of the pastel. Most pastels are too soft to be sharpened with a knife or blade, but can be rubbed carefully on a piece of sandpaper to create a point (sandpaper blocks are manufactured especially for this purpose and are available in art stores). When sharp lines and details are important. It is a good idea to give the work an occasional light spray of fixative in between stages to prevent the image from getting smudged.

4 The pale tones are applied lightly over dark blue, and the cool underpainting shows through to create a luminous and slightly unreal image *above*. Vivid strokes of color are mixed with the whites, their direction suggesting the form of the face and features.

5 Strong diagonal hatching over smooth, blended areas produces solid areas of color. Here the artist uses dense strokes of flesh-colored pastel over a dark red base *top right*.

6 The approach throughout this painting is free and uninhibited. By holding the pastel loosely and working with a broad sweeping movement of the arm, the artist produces lively strokes of broken color *right*.

John 2

What the artist used

As with the previous portrait, the artist worked from a boxed set of 24 pastels. The principal colors were white, black, violet, reds, pinks, blue, orange and flesh color. The artist worked on a sheet of primed cardboard measuring 36in×24in. A deep blue prime was chosen because the artist wanted to experiment with whites and light tones over a dark base. The work was supported on a Rowney Norwich easel, which allowed the artist to stand back from the work easily at frequent intervals. Spray fixative was used on the finished portrait.

Helen

Character and expression are important in this portrait, and the artist has relied on a quick color sketch to capture the spontaneity of the subject's smile and casual pose. The bright, warm pastel colors were used in a quick, vigorous manner, to develop the texture and main features of the portrait, rather than in the more intricate methods of some other media. For this picture, there was no preliminary bold outline, with proportions later worked in. Instead, the artist began with a light outline in burnt sienna, and the backward and forward action of the pastel quickly established the main areas, bringing the image up almost as though it were emerging through a mist, as a whole entity. Pastels can often have this rapid and direct effect if used with confidence.

Blue-gray pastel paper, which has a greenish hue in the final result, has been used as the support, giving an immediate fullness to the background, but the tint has not been allowed to overwhelm it and make it appear flat and dull. The composition of the portrait has been worked out with much more care than its spontaneous appearance indicates. Firstly, the subject was deliberately posed to one side, avoiding a rigid symmetry and adding to the seeming casualness by the slightly leaning posture. Secondly, the artist has blocked in an area of blue background in one corner, offsetting the tint and complementing the blue of the subject's clothing.

After establishing a quick outline the artist worked into the face with bright orange, ultramarine and pink and then stroked in light tones of white and yellow to firm up the main parts. In some areas the artist laid in thin strokes and then blended them by rubbing gently with a finger, a technique often used to soften the strokes of pastels. As the picture began to develop, the artist used multi-directional strokes, reinforcing the fleeting, "quick frozen" effect of the whole picture, and the face was highlighted with warm and bright tones.

SOLID AREAS OF PASTEL STROKES

Pure dense color can be built up by using tightly packed, regular strokes of pastel. Here the artist develops the face with strong, warm tones, keeping the strokes close and parallel to produce an area of solid color. Notice how the tinted paper has been virtually obliterated by the close and overlapping marks. The strokes of pure color are not blended, so that each new color stands separately from those already applied. For every strong, dense color, such as the highlights on the hair and face, the artist applies considerable pressure while drawing.

1 A quick sketch is often more successful than a carefully worked, labored drawing. This lively portrait sketch, *right,* was completed in one short sitting.

2 The outline of the head and figure are drawn in burnt sienna. The artist starts to lay in very thin strokes of warm and cool colors, blending these with the finger *top*.

3 Using the pastel lightly, the artist worked into the face with lines of bright orange, pink, and ultramarine. The hair is established with loose strokes of raw umber *above*.

4 *Above*, a regular zigzag stroke establishes the light side of the face in white and yellow. Blue and orange are worked into the shaded areas of the face, and the artist marks in a small amount of blue background tone.

5 Fine black lines and patches of strong color accentuate the shapes in the face. Outlines are redrawn in darker tones, and the flesh colors are heightened with light pink and mauve against dark red shadows *right*.

What the artist used

The artist worked on a piece of blue-gray pastel paper measuring 11in×15in. This allowed the warm, light tones of the flesh and hair to be established against the tinted paper, the cool paper color to be used to represent shadows. The artist restricted the number of pastels to 11 basic colors — black, burnt sienna, mauve, orange, pink, ultramarine blue, light blue, white, yellow, red and raw umber. A light coat of fixative was applied to the finished portrait to prevent the colors from smudging.

6 The artist looks closely at the subject, defining the darkest shadows with short, specific strokes of black. Dense white is built up on the illuminated side of the face, and the hair is developed with loose, textural strokes of black, orange, yellow, and red *above*.

7 The hand and arm are drawn with a fine black line, and then established in solid areas of pink, red, mauve, and yellow. Heavy strokes of dark blue are laid across the top of the paper to establish the background tone and to indicate space behind the subject *left*.

Helen

CHAPTER TEN

DRAWING MEDIA

Drawing with lines is the most basic means of making a picture. The term drawing covers a wide range, from rough sketches and notes to analytical studies and finished, detailed portraits. Sometimes a drawing is intended as a complete statement in its own right, and sometimes it is an early stage in a larger project, a preparation for a painting. The quality of a drawing cannot be judged by the amount of work and time involved; indeed, a rapidly drawn impression often has a liveliness and spontaneity lacking in a lengthy study, which can look rather dead.

One of the major problems of drawing is knowing how to put down what is in front of you, or how much of it to put down. Learning to draw is rather like developing a personal shorthand system, and this must become almost automatic if it is to be really successful. The actual drawing technique you evolve is irrelevant — the most important thing is that it fulfills the function for which it is required. Just as an architect's plan includes the information necessary to build or restore a house, so an artist's drawing should contain relevant visual information about a particular subject — whether as a complete work or as a reference for use in a future painting.

There is an enormous range of drawing materials now available. Alongside the traditional media, such as graphite pencil, charcoal and ink, is a vast selection of new items. In this chapter we have introduced a few of these. The Rapidograph pen, normally associated with technical work and design, is used for the portrait drawing on page 157, while colored pencils, at one time the sole preserve of children, were the artist's choice for the drawings on pages 168 and 171 . Your own selection of materials will depend to a large extent on which medium you feel comfortable with, how you work, and the reason for your drawing.

STICKS OF WILLOW CHARCOAL

CHARCOAL CRAYON

Materials

Learning to draw gives you a wide choice of materials, most of which are easily obtainable and relatively inexpensive. Each medium has its own characteristics, opening up a particular range of possible effects. If you are unaccustomed to drawing, it may be wise to start with a simple pen or pencil instead of letting yourself be seduced by the huge variety of materials available. The most extensive range of equipment is no substitute for getting down to the business of learning to draw.

Eventually, of course, as you develop your own style, you will want to experiment and to broaden your horizons. The following pages will introduce you to the various drawing media and give you an idea of their potential.

CONTE CRAYONS

Supports
The most usual support for drawing is paper, and there is a wide range of colors, textures and weights available to suit most drawing media. You can also choose between books or pads, some of which are small enough to carry around in your pocket, and large sheets for use on a drawing board. Good-quality drawing paper is made from rags and comes in linen and cotton.

CRAYON IN HOLDER

Pencil
The lead, or graphite, pencil is the most common and accessible of all drawing equipment. Most of us have been familiar with it since early schooldays, and we do not need to "learn" how to use it. The lead comes in varying degrees of softness — a very soft lead

COLORED PENCILS

WATERCOLOR PENCILS

LEAD PENCILS

CALLIGRAPHY FELT PEN

FINE FIBER PEN

BRUSH PEN

enables you to make broad, soft lines, whereas hard leads are generally used for fine, precise lines and detail.

The most common categories run as follows, from the very hard to the very soft: 8H, 7H, 6H, 5H, 4H, 3H, 2H, H, HB, F, B, 2B, 3B, 4B, 5B, 6B, 7B. The majority of H pencils are for technical or office work. The B and 2B are probably the most popular and easy to use for drawing, and you would be well advised to start with these. There is no "right" way to use a pencil, but with practice you will quickly develop your own techniques.

Also available are extremely soft pencils which sometimes have a flattened lead, and which are outside the above range. These produce dark, tonal drawing which is especially effective on rough, granular paper.

Pen and ink

This satisfying and flexible medium is as popular today as it was centuries ago, and the traditional dip-pen has changed little over the years. With this old-fashioned pen you can vary the line — something that is impossible with the modern ballpoints and felt-tips, which produce regular lines. Many artists prefer the dip-pen for this reason, but there is no reason why you should not try both types. The modern pens are certainly more convenient for sketching trips because you do not need to carry a bottle of ink around with you.

The most vital part of the equipment is the nib. It is a good idea to obtain a variety of these to see which suit your particular needs. A fountain pen is handy for outdoor work.

There is an ever-increasing range of felt- and fiber-tipped pens and markers on the market. Some have a flexible tip intended to

PLASTIC ERASER

SANDPAPER BLOCK

CRAFT KNIFE

CONTE CRAYON HOLDER

PUTTY ERASER

149

JAPANESE INK STICKS

JAPANESE BRUSHES

DIPPERS FROM DRAWING INK BOTTLES

produce an effect similar to that made with a brush and water-color, but the majority make even, uncompromising lines, and many artists dislike them for this reason. However, they are convenient, disposable and easy to carry around.

Charcoal and conté crayon

For large, tonal drawings charcoal is unbeatable. It is of particular value to the beginner because, being a solid, chunky medium, it forces an awareness of the main characteristics and form of the subject. Charcoal makes it impossible to become distracted by trivial detail, directing you instead toward the bold essentials. It is particularly useful for roughing out the composition prior to painting with oils or acrylics. It can be used on primed canvas or board, is easy to rub out and correct, and can be rubbed down to a faint outline which does not mix with the color of the paint.

You can buy charcoal made from either willow or vine. It also comes in pencil form or as compressed sticks, although these are harder than the natural charcoal.

The best eraser for charcoal is a kneaded rubber eraser. This rubs out easily and can be used to lighten tones, for blending and for drawing lighter shapes into dark areas already toned with charcoal. Charcoal tends to smudge while you are working on it, so take care. When your drawing is complete, spray it with a fixative to prevent further smudging.

For tonal drawing, use charcoal on white paper. This will enable you to exploit the extreme contrast between lights and darks. As with pastel, rough paper is best for this because the soft charcoal tends to slide off a smooth surface. Using charcoal with white chalk will enable you to work highlights into the drawing.

A similar effect can be obtained with conté crayon. This is usually sold in broad sticks, which are unsuitable for detailed work, but is also made in pencil form. Conté is harder than charcoal, being molded from a mixture of graphite, clay and paste, which makes it easier to manage but more difficult to erase. It is usually available in black, white, sepia and a brownish-red.

DIP PENS

COLORED INKS

NIB UNITS FROM
ROTRING TECHNICAL PENS

SMALL SYNTHETIC ROUND

COLORED PAPERS

SYNTHETIC FLAT

Colored pencils

Colored pencils are a very useful sketching and drawing tool, producing a compromise between a lead line-drawing and a painted image. Although their range is more limited than oil, acrylic or watercolor, new sets are coming onto the market all the time, and they are now an established artists' material instead of merely a children's toy.

Colored pencils are softer than lead pencils, but are more difficult to rub out. Mistakes usually have to be scraped off the paper with a sharp blade. Colors cannot be pre-mixed as with paints, but you can mix them "optically" on the paper by lightly overlaying different colors to obtain a rich range of combined colors.

Watercolor pencils

Watercolor pencils are a comparatively new medium which is available in an increasingly wide range. These are a cross between colored pencils and watercolor paints. Apply them in the normal way, then use a fine sable brush dipped in clean water to blend the colors together, thus creating the effect of watercolor. This is a surprisingly flexible medium, allowing you to produce tightly controlled work with well-sharpened pencils and a fine sable brush or, alternatively, to create rugged, textural areas of spontaneous pencil marks and loose washes.

Technical pens

Technical pens have a tubular nib and are specially designed for creating lines of an even thickness. They are particularly good for drawing that involves shading with hatching and cross-hatching. Many artists feel that this is a rather unsympathetic medium, but it need not necessarily be so; the success of a technical pen drawing depends very much on the style and attitude of the artist using it.

WATERCOLOR
PAPERS

SKETCHING NIBS FROM FOUNTAIN PENS

DRAWING PAPER

A White-haired Gentleman

This drawing of a man with a crisp, executive look has been done in colored and ordinary graphite pencils. The artist worked from a small photograph, beginning with a light preliminary sketch in which he mapped out some outlines of the major tonal areas.

The artist moved straight to the flesh tones of the face, first blocking in the shaded side with brown. Then he worked slowly across the features, developing each one in some detail and working back to blend each new color into some of those already established. The image was allowed to grow without too much planning or thought, this artist being very experienced in the highly graphic, instant approach. Many artists would find it quite difficult to work across an image in this way, and the less experienced would be advised to pay more attention to the overall related tones in the initial stages, possibly switching from one area to another, bringing the tones up together in relation to each other, and adjusting as the work progressed.

However, if you wish to preserve the crisp clarity of colored pencils, it is necessary to know when to stop. Two or three layers of lightly hatched color will blend happily to produce a new color; but the result can look gray, shiny and clogged if this is overdone. In this portrait, the artist solved this problem by developing each area separately, returning only for very minor adjustments.

The subject's white hair was established by leaving the surface of the white paper to show through. Its shape was defined by the pale blue-gray background which was more densely cross-hatched around the outline of the hair. The same cross-hatched background was used to define the sharp edge of the white shirt and the light side of the man's face.

1 This portrait is done from a small photograph *right.*

2 The artist starts by making a very light preliminary sketch, establishing outlines as well as defining major tonal areas. Because the reference is tiny, the artist occasionally finds it necessary to draw from experience and memory in order to make the drawing as tight as possible. When the drawing is complete, color is added an area at a time *right.* Yellow, brown, red, and black are used for the initial flesh tones around the eye.

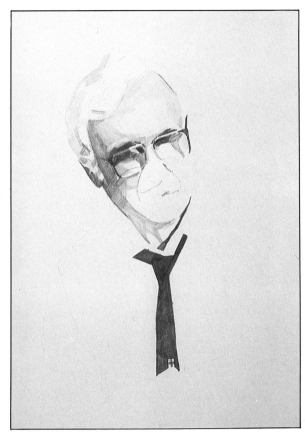

3 Cool hair shadows are added in blue *above*. The artist uses a well-sharpened pencil, working in regular hatched strokes to create darker tones.

4 Overlaid patches of blue are laid to build up the dense, dark color of the man's tie *right*. Shadows on the neck and around the eyes are darkened to accommodate this.

OVERLAYING COLOR

You can obtain any color you need with colored pencils by blending two or more colors together. Apply the first color in light regular strokes, keeping the color as even as possible — if the pencil is used too heavily other colors cannot be laid on top. Lay the second color in the same way, taking the pencil strokes in the opposite direction. If you use too many colors, the translucent quality of the blended color will be spoilt. The top color will usually be the dominant one. For instance, if you lay red over blue, the result will be a red-purple or maroon, whereas blue on top of red will produce a blue-purple.

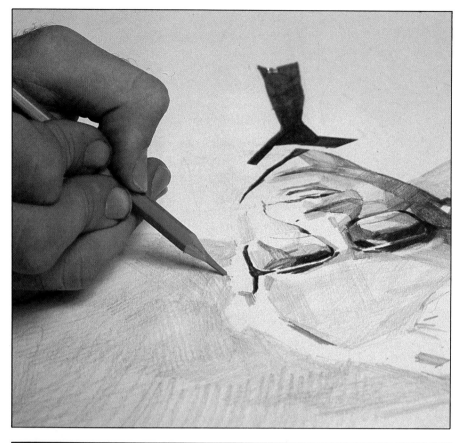

5 The artist blocks in the background with light gray, applying color in a series of cross-hatched areas of irregular tone *left*. The artist does not create deeper tones by pressing harder — instead he uses a light, even stroke, darkening the color by building up extra layers of hatching and cross-hatching.

6 White areas are represented by the whiteness of the paper. Here, the artist has taken the gray background up the edge of the white hair and shirt, carefully preserving the outlines and defining them as negative shapes *above*.

7 The artist develops the background, adding blue to pick out the blue tones in the figure *left*. The side of the pencil is used here to soften the cross-hatching and to cover the area more quickly.

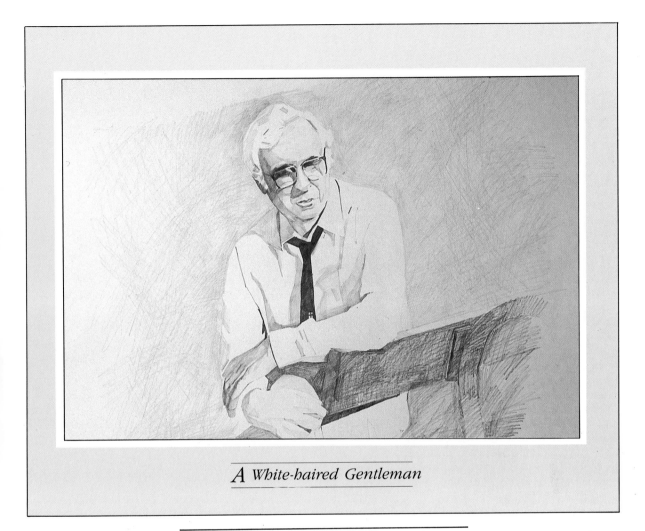

A White-haired Gentleman

What the artist used

For this colored pencil drawing, the artist worked on a sheet of drawing paper measuring 30in×20in. The colors selected were brown, red, yellow, black, dark blue, light blue and light gray. Other colors were mixed "optically" from this basic set by careful overlaying (for example, red and brown are combined in some of the facial shadows to produce a warm mahogany tone). A craft knife was kept at hand, and the pencils were frequently sharpened throughout to maintain the fine cross-hatching and delicate lines.

Maurice

A technical pen, which has been used for this portrait, can be a very unrelenting medium. The line produced is of a consistent, even thickness; it is impossible to achieve the natural undulating movement of a brush or pen-and-ink line. However, here the artist has used the pen in conjunction with the more sympathetic effect of a soft Chinese brush. The advantages of a technical pen are that you do not have to keep stopping to refill it, there is a wide choice of nibs, and once mastered, it is more flexible than it immediately appears. The artist sketched out the basic outline with the pen's even line, but then varied this by keeping the drawing loose and by working over areas to produce different textures and a sense of liveliness. The drawing has been kept very rounded and flowing.

The artist did not just draw the outline and then change to the brush, but used the two tools alternately, blending some areas of the drawing with water and thin color as the work progressed. Ordinary sepia fountain-pen ink was used for this. In some cases, lines were altered after being placed on the paper — a technique which many people do not realize is possible when using pens. There are two kinds of ink — waterproof and water-soluble — and the artist used the soluble kind, which meant that lines could be practically rubbed out with water after being applied, and even after they dried. This gave a flexibility to the process. In cases where lines did not totally disappear, as on Maurice's corrected collar, the presence of a new, redrawn line knocked the original line back sufficiently for it not to be noticed. At one stage, the artist changed the position of the eyebrow by dissolving the original line with water applied with the brush.

Although this artist used ordinary ink, this is not generally advisable when working with technical pens. Specially prepared inks can be obtained for the fine tubular nibs; these makes contain a solvent which prevents the ink from drying and clogging the tube — a mishap that sometimes renders the pen impossible to clean.

2 To soften the effect of the regular technical line, the artist works on slightly damp paper *above*. This causes the ink to bleed slightly, producing a runny, irregular line.

1 The amiable expression on the man's face, *right,* was captured in a quick sepia ink sketch using a Chinese brush and technical pen.

CHINESE BRUSHES

Chinese brushes are softer than ordinary watercolor brushes. They have fine hairs and are useful for soft, irregular washes and creating delicate flecks of color. Here the artist uses the brush with water to soften the hard pen lines and to create a wash with the released sepia color.

3 The artist drags a wet Chinese brush across the neck and hair lines, *left,* blurring the outline, and causing those areas to recede. This emphasizes the sharpness of the facial features, and creates a sense of form and depth in the drawing.

4 As the drawing develops, the artist strives to maintain a balance between the crisp precision of the technical drawing and the soft wash effects of the brushwork *left*.

What the artist used

For this portrait the artist worked on drawing paper measuring 18in×13in with a technical pen and sepia ink. She used a Chinese brush to soften the lines.

Maurice

John in Black and White

When working in black and white it is often helpful to choose a medium-colored support. This enables you to start working in both black and white from the start, as both will register equally clearly against the middle tone. This portrait has been done in black and white chalk. The artist, who is an illustrator and usually works in watercolor on a small scale, enjoyed this opportunity to experiment in a bold way in a different medium.

She worked very quickly, straight on the paper, chalking loosely and trying to familiarize herself with the appearance of the model. Right away, she began to block in the large contrasting areas of tone, starting with a very broad white approximation of the position of the model's face, and building on the image in both black and white, creating space and a three-dimensional form. She took advantage of the dense opaque quality that chalk has when used boldly, laying in large areas without worrying about whether she was making mistakes, but going ahead and adjusting as she worked.

The tonal planes of the face are rubbed together to blend the contrasting blacks and whites into the soft, rounded contours of the human features. Because she was working on a large scale she found it necessary to use her whole hand to blend the larger areas together to obtain this softer gray medium tone.

One advantage of working with chalks is that lines and tones can be easily changed as you work, so the artist was able to let herself go, confident that no statement was irreversible. She was able to work instinctively, but once the very loose basics were established her drawing became more disciplined and controlled. Details of the face were applied using a combination of finer lines and broad strokes.

Chalk drawings must be fixed, because the loose powder is easily rubbed off the surface of the paper, blurring the image. In this picture the artist not only fixed the final image, she also used a light spray of fixative over the earlier stages of the work, preparing it for finishing touches. If you do use fixative before the finished work is ready, it must be extra light — fixative is actually a varnish and the chalk will slide over a very hard surface.

2 Working on a large sheet of blue tinted paper, the artist immediately starts to block in some of the main areas of dark and light *above*.

1 There is no significant color in the subject *right*. For the artist, the interest lies in the tones — the arrangement of lights and darks.

3 The edge of the chalk is used to block in large areas quickly *right*. Bold wedges of black and white are quickly established in this way.

4 The artist uses her hands to blend large areas as she works *left*. Blending is used to strengthen the image and to obliterate some of the blue paper, which shows through and weakens the image. The portrait is essentially sketchy and spontaneous, and no attempt is made to refine or change the character of the strong textural chalk marks.

BLENDING

Like pastel, chalk and charcoal can be blended by rubbing the two together or by laying one over the other. Here the artist uses the side of the sticks to apply black over white to create a broad area of middle tone. In the second picture she uses her fingers to blend the black and white into a smooth gray. A soft kneaded eraser can also be useful for rubbing back large areas of chalk or charcoal to reveal the support color underneath.

5 Although small areas of blue paper can be seen, the drawing is emphatically black and white. The artist used the tone of the paper as a starting point only, relating the initial strokes of light and dark to this convenient middle tone. In the picture so far, *right,* we see how these sharply contrasting tones have taken over. The direction of the chalk strokes on the solid tonal blocks describes the form of the figure; graphic black and white shapes dominate the composition.

6 To preserve the sharp tonal contrasts and to prevent smudging the artist sprays the finished drawing with fixative *above*. Holding the can about a foot away from the paper, she sprays from side to side, gradually moving downward, until the whole support is covered.

John in Black and White

What the artist used

The artist used black and white chalk on a sheet of blue Ingres paper measuring 24in×18in. By using tinted paper the artist was able to use black and white immediately to establish the light and dark tones of the portrait. She used a drawing board supported on a Rowney Norwich easel. The completed drawing was given a coat of spray fixative.

Woman in Red and White Chair

The artist has drawn surrounding elements into this picture, making the portrait an elegant and individual interpretation of the subject. The wrought-iron table with its distinctive twining shapes adds formality to this colored-pencil portrait, as well as breaking major rules about composition. For instance, the composition is divided vertically into two equal halves by the background division. It is also split horizontally by the line of the table top. However, within this unlikely symmetrical system, a harmonious composition has been created. The flowing lines and curves of the subject and the chair are so dominant and so very different from the uncompromising composition grid that they offset any uncomfortable rigidity. Color also plays a role in the composition. The red chair and the red clothing are the only strong colors in the picture, and this focuses the eye on the soft, easy contours of both the figure and the chair.

A very simple light pencil drawing acted as a minimal guide for color and stronger contrasting tones. This artist often starts with the head when working in portraiture, since this is the main feature, and he prefers to establish this early in the process. He developed a considerable amount of detail in the head and hands by laying one color over another. He applied a main color and then modified this by a light top layer of a second tone. On the face, for instance, he laid down a local color of flesh pink, working a thin layer of brown over this to produce a deeper tone of the local color. Hence he achieved something of the transparency of the glazing process used in oils or acrylic.

The artist drew in the red skirt using loose strokes, building up the darker shadow areas by overlaying the same color to obtain a denser tone. Again, brown pencil was used to create the darkest tones of the folds. The stripes on the chair were drawn freely, judged their position, by eye carefully following the form of the chair, rather than by any method of mechanical measurement.

1 The artist liked this arrangement of the woman sitting in the striped chair at the table, *right*.

2 Working on white drawing paper, the artist starts by making a light line drawing with an F pencil (this preliminary drawing is very accurate, leaving the artist free to concentrate on color and tone). The hair is blocked in with black, the denseness of the cross-hatching determining the depth of tone and helping to establish form. Black and brown are combined to establish the shadows around the eyes *right*.

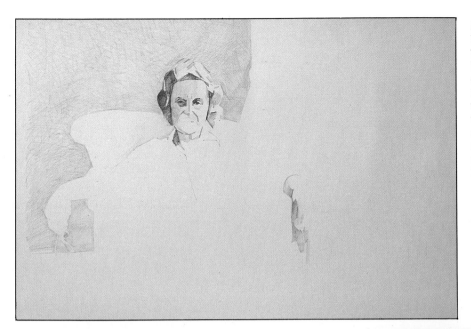

3 Flesh tones are built up from brown, yellow ocher and gray. The artist blends pencil colors by carefully cross-hatching one color over another. At this stage, the background is blocked in with pale gray *left*. This is done with a combination of tight cross-hatching and loose scribbling, giving textural variation to the large background expanse.

4 The artist puts in the red skirt, building up layers of cross-hatching to create the dense color of the shadows and folds in the material. Very dark shadows are over-hatched with brown *above*.

5 Here, *right,* the artist draws the red stripes of the chair in crimson red. The stripes, filled in with neat directional pencil strokes, describe the curved form of the chair. Highlights are indicated by lighter color.

HATCHING AND CROSS-HATCHING

Depth and areas of dark tone can be created by hatching and cross-hatching. Apply the pencil in neat, directional strokes (hatching), and build up the tone with overlaid strokes in the opposite direction (cross-hatching). Here the artist is using several layers of black to build up the deep shadows and recessed shapes of the subject's hair.

Keep the pencils well sharpened and apply each layer systematically to give yourself maximum control over the texture and depth of tone.

6 Background details are added with as much precision as in the main subject. The warm red tones of the face and lips are emphasized by the strong red stripes of the same color *top*.

7 The artist uses the direction of the pencil strokes to describe form. Notice how the strokes on the arm, hand, and chair follow the contours *above*.

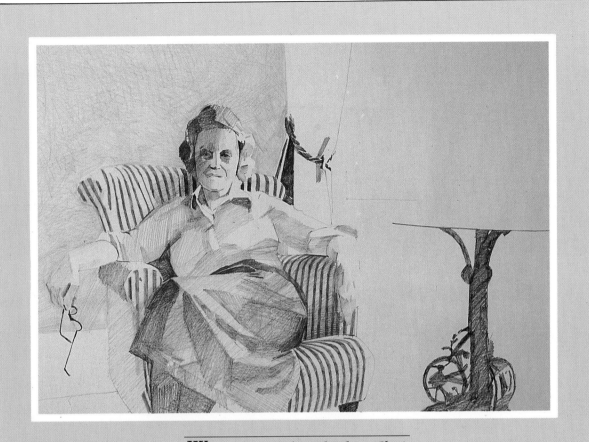

Woman in Red and White Chair

What the artist used

The support for this portrait drawing was a sheet of white drawing paper measuring approximately 22in×18in. White paper was chosen because the artist wanted to use this to regulate the tones of the drawing — for example, to create pink, it is possible to hatch well-spaced red lines, with the width of the white spaces between them determining the tone of the final color. He also used the white paper to represent highlights. The basic colors were black, gray, red, crimson, yellow, burnt sienna, and brown. A preliminary drawing was done with an F pencil, and the colored pencils were sharpened with a craft knife.

Sunlit Face

The face basks in sunlight, and the artist has set out to capture it — both in mood and in visual tones of light — in a pen-and-ink portrait. The direct playing of the light on the face gives the artist the opportunity to indicate this by means of strongly contrasting areas of light and shade.

The support for this portrait was white drawing paper, and therefore light could be depicted in "negative" fashion, by leaving areas of the white paper untouched. The artist, in fact, was observing light by drawing shade, an ideal task for pen and ink. But this is not as simple as it may sound, for the areas of shade vary delicately from light to dark, established in this case by grading the density of the inked lines and dots.

Working directly on an expanse of white can seem daunting, but the artist here used a light pencil outline as a guide, concentrating on the profile of the head. This outline was to be used only as a reference, showing where shadow and highlighted areas were to be developed.

The artist moved the pen vigorously, producing lively strokes and avoiding the stiffness which can sometimes result from pen and ink. Making initial use of the pencil guide, the artist hatched a dark tone on one side of the head to throw the profile into relief. Notice that the artist resisted the temptation to mark out the complete profile, leaving blank space between the bottom of the nose and the mouth, and the chin below the mouth. These features were to be brought clearly into silhouette later by hatching in background areas of shadow. Next the artist created an immediate feeling of mood by some touches of the pen which established the relaxed positions of the eye and mouth. Again, more detail was to be worked into these parts later.

Using fine parallel lines slanted across the paper, the artist next developed shadows inside the shape of the head and then worked outward into the background in the same way. Some areas were cross-hatched to darken them, and gradually the image spread across the whole paper.

Stippling with the nib of the pen was used in the final stages to add detail to the texture and shadow in the face. The effect of strong sunlight was maintained by developing a high contrast of light and dark down the face and body. It was important to keep this in mind from the start, and to avoid overdoing the pen-work which would otherwise have produced a grayer effect and the "sunlit" look would have been lost.

1 A well-lit profile, *right,* can capture characteristics as successfully as the more traditional full-faced and three-quarters portrait angles.

STIPPLING

Fine shadows and texture can be created by stippling with pen and ink. Here the artist develops the facial shading with a series of tiny dots, varying the density of these to create lighter or darker shadows. The dots are used to complement the more formal cross-hatched shading, creating a marked difference between the soft, irregular texture and contours of the face and the larger, angular tonal areas elsewhere in the composition.

Above, left to right. A dark tone is hatched down the side of the head, throwing the profile into relief. Then the facial shadows and background are developed with fine diagonal lines — white paper is left to represent the bright highlights. In the next picture, working across the whole drawing, the artist works into the shadows, developing these in relation to each other. Finally, the background tones are expanded to cover more of the paper. Head and clothes are developed with small, detailed patterns.

What the artist used

A dip pen with a medium nib was used for this pen and ink portrait. The artist worked on white drawing paper measuring 10in×11½in with black waterproof India ink.

Sunlit Face

The Chinese Gown

This portrait is almost a monochrome study in black and white, except for the Naples yellow of the skin and background, yet its most immediate impact on the viewer is made by the colorful pattern of the Chinese gown. This has been established by working in comparatively small blocks of local color. The starkness of the basic color scheme gives the picture a stylized look, almost like a printed illustration which has been reproduced in a restricted number of colors. It is not unlike a fashion illustration. This feeling is strengthend by the background, which consists of a stylish vase of flowers which the artist has included in a very basic, almost symbolic form.

The skin tones here have been unusually observed, and local color is important. The shadows are predominantly in gray and black with the highlights in pure white.

The drawing was done quickly. Time was limited, and the artist had to make rapid decisions about what information to record and what to discard. Color is used simply and graphically in bold pure areas.

It is the black shape of the hair and gown which holds this composition together. These are established with confidence, the pencil strokes alone indicating the direction of the form. The hair, for instance, is built up by overlapping a mass of dark strokes and allowing the white paper to show through in areas affected by the light. Facial tones are described in more detail but still in the same emphatic directional strokes.

The artist began by making a basic drawing, using a dark-brown colored pencil. This linear drawing was developed as the blocking-in progressed, and each area was quite firmly indicated in the early stages. Although the drawing is minimal, the line has a tautness and discipline which is the result of careful observation and accurate work.

The difference in surface textures of the drawing is suggested by a varied and creative use of hatching and cross-hatching. The background, for example, is established as an area of black cross-hatching over an undercolor of yellow. This light evenness contrasts with both the lively scribbled fabric of the gown and the smoothly rendered flesh tones.

1 The model, leaning against the arm of a sofa, *right,* looks directly at the artist as she sketches her portrait.

2 Using a dark brown pencil, the artist starts by sketching in the composition and the position of the figure. Here, *top,* she draws in the head.

3 The face and features are established in light strokes of brown. Hair tones are blocked in with black *above.*

4 Hair is built up with overlapping masses of dark strokes, allowing white paper to show through in areas affected by light *left*. The artist works quickly and accurately, attempting to draw each line as a final statement, instead of anticipating subsequent change.

5 The smooth drawing paper allows the pencil to glide smoothly over the surface *below*. Lack of texture on the paper surface is compensated for by the strong directional pencil strokes which the artist uses to block in areas of color and tone.

DIRECTIONAL PENCIL STROKES

The direction of the pencil strokes can play an important part in describing form. Because pencil is essentially a linear medium it can be difficult and time-consuming to suggest large forms through light and shade. Here the artist has carefully used the direction of the strokes to help indicate such form. The material on the gown is sketchily treated, but the loose drawing follows the direction of the folds of the garment to show the underlying forms of the subject's arms, shoulders and chest. The hair is not treated as a solid shape, but is built up from lines of color that follow the fall of the hair.

6 Fine hatching brings out the modeling on the face *above*. Apart from the local flesh tint there is no actual color in the face. Shading is restricted to gray and black; highlights are represented by white paper.

7 The patterned robe is heavily blocked in with bold colors *above*. In order to cover this comparatively large area, the artist works quickly with broad directional pencil strokes.

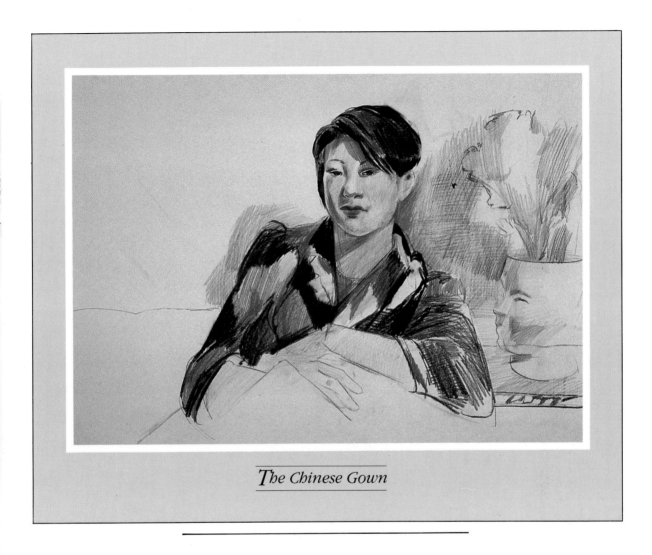

The Chinese Gown

What the artist used

This rapid colored pencil portrait was sketched on a sheet of white drawing paper measuring 15in×20in. The artist used a selection of colors, including black, dark gray, yellow, red, dark blue, light blue, brown, violet, and bright green. Colored pencils form a compromise between a lead line drawing and a colored painting. Their color range is more restricted than oils, acrylics, or gouache, but new sets with an increasingly wide choice of colors are appearing continually and are gaining in popularity. Although the colors cannot be pre-mixed, as with paints, they can be mixed "optically" on the paper by overlaying different colors to obtain a wide range of colors.

Glossary

ABSTRACT Relying on color and form rather than the realistic or naturalistic portrayal of subject matter.

ABSTRACTION The creation of an abstract image from a subject or other figurative reference.

ACRYLIC A comparatively new paint in which the pigment is suspended in a synthetic resin. It is quick-drying, permanent, and colorfast.

ADVANCING COLORS Colors that appear to stand out, because they are brighter, stronger or denser than their neighbors.

AERIAL PERSPECTIVE The use of color and tone to denote space and distance.

ALLA PRIMA Direct painting in which the picture is completed in one session without any underpainting or underdrawing.

BINDER Any liquid medium that forms a paint when mixed with powder pigment.

BLENDING Merging colors together in such a way that the joins are imperceptible.

BLOCKING-IN The initial stage of a painting when the main forms and composition are laid down in approximate areas of color and tone.

BROKEN COLOR Paint applied in its pure state rather than being mixed. This stiff paint is usually applied by dragging the brush across the surface, allowing layers of color underneath to show through.

CHIAROSCURO The exploitation of light and shadow within a painting. Both Caravaggio and Rembrandt were masters of the technique.

COLLAGE A picture made up from pieces of paper, fabric, and other materials glued onto canvas, paper, or some other support.

COMPOSITION The arrangement and combination of different elements to make a picture.

COMPLEMENTARY COLORS Colors that appear opposite each other in the color circle. Hence, purple is complementary to yellow, green to red, and orange to blue.

COVERING POWER This refers to the opacity of a paint — its ability to obliterate the color underneath.

CROSS-HATCHING A method of building up areas of shadow with layers of criss-cross lines rather than with solid tone.

FIXATIVE Thin varnish which is sprayed on drawing media, especially charcoal and pastel, to prevent smudging and to protect the surface.

FRESCO A wall-painting usually done with watercolor on damp plaster.

GLAZING Painting a transparent film of color over another pigment.

GROUND A ground is painted onto a surface to make the surface suitable for painting on. With oil painting, for instance, the ground is usually gesso or an oil-based mixture.

GUM ARABIC Used with watercolor and inks to give body and sheen. Obtained from a species of acacia.

GUM WATER A solution of gum arabic used with inks and watercolors to provide extra sheen and body.

HATCHING A shading technique which uses parallel lines instead of solid tones to build up form.

HUE A tint or shade.

IMPASTO The thick application of paint or pastel to the picture surface in order to create texture.

LEAN A term used to describe oil color that has little or no added oil. The term "fat over lean" refers to the traditional method of using "lean" color (paint thinned with turpentine or mineral spirit) in the early stages of a painting and working over this with "fat," or oil paint, as the painting progresses.

LINEAR PERSPECTIVE A system for drawing space and objects in space on a two-dimensional surface. It is based on the fact that parallel lines going in any one direction appear to meet at a point on the horizon. This point is referred to as the vanishing point.

LOCAL COLOR The actual color of the surface of an object without modification by light, shade or distance.

MASK A device used to prevent paint or any other medium from affecting the picture surface in order to retain the color of the support or the existing paint in a particular area.

MASKING The principle of blocking out areas of a painting to retain the color of the support. This is usually done with tape or masking fluid and leaves the artist free to paint over the masked areas. The masks are removed when the paint is dry to reveal the areas underneath.

MASKING FLUID A rubber solution which is painted onto a picture surface to retain the color of the paper or support. When the solution is dry, the artist can paint safely over the masked areas. The mask is removed by rubbing it with an eraser or finger.

MEDIUM In a general sense the medium is the type of material used, such as oil paint or charcoal. More specifically, a medium is a substance mixed with paint or pigment for a particular purpose or to obtain a certain effect.

MIXED MEDIA The technique of using two or more established media, such as ink and gouache, in the same picture.

MONOCHROME A painting done using black, white and one other color.

NEGATIVE SPACE The space around the subject rather than the subject itself.

OPACITY The ability of a pigment to cover and obscure the surface or color to which it is applied.

OPTICAL MIXING Mixing color in the painting rather than on the palette. For example, using dabs of red and yellow to give the illusion of orange rather than applying a pre-mixed orange.

PICTURE PLANE That area of a picture that lies directly behind the frame and separates the viewer's world from that of the picture.

PLANES The surface areas of the subject which can be seen in terms of light and shade.

PRIMARY COLORS In painting these are red, blue and yellow. They cannot be obtained from any other colors.

PRIMER The first coat on the support over which other layers — including the ground — are laid.

RENAISSANCE The cultural revival of classical ideals that took place in the fifteenth and sixteenth centuries.

RENDER To draw or reproduce an image.

SATURATED COLOR Color with a high degree of purity. The degree of saturation is assessed by comparing it with a colorless area of equal brightness.

SIZE A gelatinous solution such as rabbit skin glue which is used to prepare the surface of the canvas or board ready for priming or painting.

STENCIL A piece of cardboard or other material out of which patterns have been cut. The pattern or motif is made by painting through the hole.

STIPPLE Painting, drawing or engraving using dots instead of line or flat color. A special brush is available for stippling paint.

SUPPORT A surface for painting or drawing on, usually canvas, board or paper.

TORTILLON A stump used for blending charcoal and pastel. This is often made of rolled paper or chamois.

UNDERDRAWING A preliminary drawing for a painting, often done in pencil, charcoal or paint.

UNDERPAINTING The preliminary blocking-in of the basic colors, the structure of a painting, and its tonal values.

WASH An application of ink or watercolor, diluted to make the color spread transparently and evenly.

WET-INTO-DRY The application of paint to a completely dry surface causing the sharp overlapping shapes to create the impression of structured form.

WET-INTO-WET The application of paint to a surface that is still wet to create a subtle blending of color.

Index

Credits

Quarto would like to thank all those who have helped in the preparation of this book. We would like to thank all the artists, with special thanks to Daler-Rowney for their patience and generosity in donating materials and items of equipment.

Contributing artists
p *20*, Maurice Wilson; pp *20-23, 33* (*left* and *bottom left*) Stan Smith; pp *80-83*, Gordon Bennett; pp *130-133*, Margaret Clarke; pp *120-123, 168-171*, John Devane; pp *24* (*top right*), *100-107, 116-119, 124-125, 134-141*, Elaine Mills; pp *24* (*top left* and *bottom right*), *52-55, 56-59, 64-65, 70-79, 90-93, 108-111, 146-147, 152-155, 162-165*, Ian Sidaway; pp *40-41, 46-51, 60-63*, Wendy Shrimpton; pp *24* (*bottom right*), *112-115, 156-157*, Jane Wisner; pp *94-95, 142-145*, Marc Winer

Other illustrations
p *6* National Gallery of Scotland (Sutherland loan); p *8* Courtesy of the Trustees, Courtauld Institute Galleries, London; p *9* (*above*) Courtesy of the Greater London Council as Trustees of the Iveagh Bequest, Kenwood; p *9* (*below*) Frans Halsmuseum, Haarlem, the Netherlands; p *35* The Trustees, the National Gallery, London; p *37* By permission of the National Museum of Wales; p *38* Reproduced by permission of the Trustees, the Wallace Collection, London; pp *42-45, 66-69, 96-99, 126-129, 148-151*, photography by David Burch.